Discovery & Exploration

Exploration in the
Age of Empire, 1750–1953
Revised Edition

DISCOVERY & EXPLORATION

Exploration in the World of the Ancients,
   Revised Edition

Exploration in the World of the Middle Ages,
   500–1500, Revised Edition

Exploration in the Age of Empire, 1750–1953,
   Revised Edition

Exploring the Pacific, Revised Edition

Exploring the Polar Regions, Revised Edition

Discovery of the Americas, 1492–1800,
   Revised Edition

Opening Up North America, 1497–1800,
   Revised Edition

Across America: The Lewis and Clark Expedition,
   Revised Edition

Exploring North America, 1800–1900, Revised Edition

Exploring Space, Revised Edition

Exploration in the Age of Empire, 1750–1953

Revised Edition

KEVIN PATRICK GRANT

JOHN S. BOWMAN and MAURICE ISSERMAN
General Editors

CHELSEA HOUSE
PUBLISHERS
An imprint of Infobase Publishing

Chelsea House
An imprint of Infobase Publishing
132 West 31st Street
New York NY 10001

Library of Congress Cataloging-in-Publication Data
Grant, Kevin Patrick.
  Exploration in the age of empire, 1750–1953 / by Kevin Patrick Grant. – Rev. ed.
     p. cm. – (Discovery and exploration)
  Includes bibliographical references and index.
  ISBN 978-1-60413-189-5 (hardcover)
  1. Discoveries in geography–European–Juvenile literature. I. Title. II. Series.
  G133.G67 2009
  910.94'0903--dc22
                                    2009022108

Chelsea House books are available at special discounts when purchased in bulk quantities for businesses, associations, institutions, or sales promotions. Please call our Special Sales Department in New York at (212) 967-8800 or (800) 322-8755.

You can find Chelsea House on the World Wide Web at
http://www.chelseahouse.com

Text design by Erika K. Arroyo
Cover design by Keith Trego

Printed in the United States of America

Bang EJB 10 9 8 7 6 5 4 3 2 1

This book is printed on acid-free paper.

All links and Web addresses were checked and verified to be correct at the time of publication. Because of the dynamic nature of the Web, some addresses and links may have changed since publication and may no longer be valid.

Contents

1

"Dr. Livingstone, I Presume?"

On July 15, 1871, Dr. David Livingstone, the most famous British explorer of the nineteenth century, stood on the banks of the Lualaba River in central Africa. For three months he had watched the river flow slowly into the heart of Africa. He was desperate to cross, as he believed that on the other side he would discover the source of the great Nile River, but unfortunately, he and his 13 African servants had not been able to persuade anyone in the nearby town of Nyangwe to provide them with boats. Livingstone had just made his last offer— everything that he had to give. He had told one of the leading merchants, Dugumbe, that he would give him the huge sum of $2,000 and all the supplies he had stored in the distant town of Ujiji for passage across the river.

With this offer on the table, Livingstone decided to pass the time in the town's marketplace. After about an hour, he began to make his way out of the market. He noticed three men, armed with guns, arguing with one of the local African merchants over the price of a chicken. The armed men were not from Nyangwe. They were Muslims from East Africa, commonly known to Europeans of the day as Arabs. These men worked for Dugumbe, a fellow Arab. He and the armed men hoped to profit from the local slave trade and from blood feuds between Dugumbe and his enemies. "Before I had got thirty yards out," Livingstone later recalled in his journal, "the discharge of two guns in the middle of the crowd told me that slaughter had begun: crowds dashed off from the place, and threw down their wares in confusion, and ran."

David Livingstone made some of the most spectacular discoveries during his day. His explorations took him from one end of southern Africa to the other and he was the first European to see the tallest waterfall in the world, which he named Victoria Falls. In his search for the source of the Nile, he discovered several large lakes and mapped many of Africa's rivers.

The armed men opened fire upon the fleeing crowd. Another group of armed men joined in the shooting, firing at the men and women who attempted to escape in their canoes. Hundreds of people jumped into the river and began to swim for an island about a mile offshore.

Livingstone watched the long line of heads bobbing in the water. He realized with horror that the current would carry them well beyond the island and then downstream. Most would surely drown. Livingstone recalled in his journal:

> Shot after shot continued to be fired on the helpless and perishing. Some of the long line of heads disappeared quietly; while other poor creatures threw their arms high and sank. One canoe took in as many as it could hold, and all paddled with hands and arms: three canoes, got out in haste, picked up sinking friends, till all went down together and disappeared.

The people of Nyangwe had fled to escape enslavement. Many had assumed that the armed men intended to round them up, place them in chains and wooden collars, then march them to the coast to be sold. For some, even death was better than enslavement. Livingstone watched a woman in the river refuse to be rescued by Dugumbe's men in canoes. The woman drowned, as Livingstone stood helplessly on the shore.

DR. LIVINGSTONE'S DILEMMA

The slave trade in central Africa was flourishing in the mid-nineteenth century. On the Lualaba River, Muslims from the East controlled the slave trade. They abducted the Bantu peoples or purchased them from local chiefs. The slave traders then sold these people to work on coastal plantations, which specialized in the production of cloves. Some people were brought to the Arabian Peninsula and Asia, where the Africans were sold again to work as manual laborers or servants. The trade in slaves had become more difficult since the British government had abolished the slave trade and emancipated slaves throughout much of the British Empire in 1833. By mid-century, the British Royal Navy patrolled the African coasts, stopping slave ships. Ironically, as the British government pursued its antislavery policies, British and other European explorers depended upon the slave trade for their survival. They followed the age-old routes of the slave caravans and often relied on the advice and support of the same slave traders whose work they condemned.

Livingstone had begun his career in exploration as a "medical missionary," combining his skills as a physician with his efforts to convert

Africans to Christianity. He had then become an abolitionist, as those who were against slavery were called. Livingstone had regarded exploration as essential to the success of his Christian mission, thinking it would forge the path for Christian civilization to follow. He had then come to believe that exploration was essential to exposing the horrors of the slave trade. He faced a moral dilemma. Was it right for him to depend upon Dugumbe and other slave traders for his progress to the four fountains, the legendary source of the Nile?

In response to the massacre at Nyangwe, Livingstone decided to give up his attempts to cross the Lualaba, if only for the time being. He prepared to return to his base of operations at Ujiji, on the shores of Lake Tanganyika. He hoped to muster a new company of servants to accompany him in his explorations. Dugumbe and the other slave traders in the area were pleased to see Livingstone go. They knew that he had won support for his explorations by promising to investigate and expose the ongoing slave trade in Africa. Although the slave traders had helped Livingstone to survive in the jungles of Africa, they had also refused to deliver his reports and letters via their caravans to the coast. In a gesture of good faith, Dugumbe gave him gunpowder and other necessities for the journey. Livingstone accepted the supplies and left Nyangwe on July 22, 1871.

In the next several weeks, Livingstone and his African servants covered hundreds of miles. They walked on paths only as wide as a man's outstretched arms, between walls of dense jungle foliage that hid the light of day. Livingstone had several bouts of fever and steadily lost weight during the march. In a dangerous case of mistaken identity, African villagers thought that Livingstone was a slave trader. They tried to kill him in retaliation for the slave trader's brutality. In dense jungle, a spear flew closely behind Livingstone and stuck in the ground. Further on, a spear flew just a foot in front of him. Despite these and other mishaps along the way, Livingstone arrived at Ujiji on October 23. He appeared—by his own account—"a skeleton."

Soon after Livingstone's arrival, one of his employees betrayed him and sold most of Livingstone's supplies, turning a profit at Livingstone's expense. The people of Ujiji would not help Livingstone recover his supplies, and he could not count on the British government for help. The nearest British officials were hundreds of miles away. No white man had seen Livingstone in two years. It had been many months since any of his letters had reached the coast. In fact, rumors had begun to circulate in Europe and the United States that the great explorer was either lost or dead.

Livingstone was forced to live on the charity of his hosts. "This was distressing," Livingstone observed in his journal. "To wait in beggary was what I never contemplated, and I now felt miserable." It was not clear when, if ever, Livingstone would again have a chance to find the source of the Nile. It was not even clear how long he would be welcome at Ujiji, a town established and dominated by slave traders. Then, one morning, Livingstone saw his servant, Abdullah Susi, running toward him. He had urgent news. "An Englishman," Susi declared, "I see him!" The young man then dashed away.

PURSUING THE RUMOR OF LIVINGSTONE

Henry Morton Stanley was not an Englishman, but an American journalist who had been hired by the *New York Herald* to find the famous Dr. Livingstone, dead or alive. Stanley had departed from the East African coast almost eight months before. He traveled with a caravan of almost 200 African men. He and his followers had fought many battles against hostile tribes and nearly starved in the course of their grueling march. Stanley had overcome a mutiny and survived 23 attacks of fever. He was driven by a rumor that Livingstone was at Lake Tanganyika. Remarkably, at the outset of this expedition, Stanley had possessed no experience as an explorer or as a leader of men.

Stanley ordered one of his strongest servants to carry an American flag at the head of the caravan as it entered Ujiji. A large crowd of people from the town began to gather around them. In the midst of the excitement Stanley heard someone on his right say, "Good morning, sir!" Startled, Stanley turned to see a young black man. According to his own later account of this episode, Stanley asked,

"Who the mischief are you?"
"I am Susi, the servant of Dr. Livingstone," replied he, smiling.
"What! Dr. Livingstone, here?"
"Yes, sir."
"In this village?"

Henry Morton Stanley (*above*) found David Livingstone after marching for eight months through hundreds of miles of African jungle. Stanley located Livingstone by the shores of Lake Tanganyika, during which he uttered the famous phrase, "Dr. Livingstone, I presume?"

"Yes, sir."

"Are you sure?"

"Sure, sure, sir. Why, I leave him just now."

"Now, you Susi, run, and tell the Doctor I am coming."

"Yes, sir," and off he darted like a madman.

Stanley later wrote in his memoirs that he was almost mad with joy following this conversation. After eight months of hardship, he had located Livingstone. Stanley recalled:

> *What would I not have given for a bit of friendly wilderness, where, unseen, I might vent my joy in some mad freak, such as idiotically biting my hand, turning a somersault, or slashing at trees, in order to allay those exciting feelings that were well-nigh uncontrollable. My heart beats fast, but I must not let my face betray my emotions, lest it shall detract from the dignity of a white man appearing under such extraordinary circumstances.*

Stanley made his way through the crowds of people until he reached a semicircle of Arabs, before whom stood a lone white man with a gray beard. Stanley recalled:

> *I noticed he was pale, looked wearied, wore a bluish cap with a faded gold band round it, had on a red-sleeved waistcoat, and a pair of grey tweed trousers. I would have run to him, only I was a coward in the presence of such a mob; so I did what cowardice and false pride suggested was the best thing—walked deliberately to him, took off my hat, and said:*
>> *"Dr. Livingstone, I presume?"*
>> *"Yes," said he, with a kind smile, lifting his cap slightly.*

The men replaced their hats and shook hands. Stanley declared: "I thank God, Doctor, I have been permitted to see you." He answered, "I feel thankful that I am here to welcome you."

Upon speaking with Stanley, Livingstone might have heard a Welsh accent. Stanley had been born and raised in Wales before moving to the United States as a child. These two children of Great Britain had followed entirely different journeys to meet on the shore of Lake Tanganyika in 1871. Their journeys say a great deal about the larger forces that drove exploration in the age of empire.

LIVINGSTONE'S EARLY LIFE

David Livingstone was born to a working-class family in Blantyre, Scotland, in 1813. From the age of 10 until his early twenties, David worked in a local cotton mill. After work each day he attended the company school. There, he learned to read and write. He also attended Sunday school, and in his spare time he read books about travel and science. In 1834, he read a religious pamphlet asking for medical missionaries in China. Livingstone saw this as a way to pursue his interest in science and religion. It was also a way to escape life in the mill. With charitable assistance, he succeeded in enrolling in the medical school at Andersonian University in Glasgow. After completing his medical studies, Livingstone was taken on by the London Missionary Society.

Livingstone arrived at Cape Town, South Africa, in 1841. He then traveled north into the interior, where he was disappointed by the slow progress of missionary work. Livingstone believed most other missionaries in South Africa were timid, incompetent, and small-minded. They regarded him as rude and overbearing. Livingstone disagreed with many of his fellow missionaries over the potential of Africans. Whereas most missionaries characterized Africans as savage and childlike, Livingstone felt that African people possessed cultures deserving of respect as well as intelligence capable of development under the guidance of Christian civilization.

Livingstone began exploring South Africa to create distance between himself and the missionary community. He had learned to prefer Africans to Europeans as traveling companions. Most explorers of his era ruled their expeditions with an iron fist. Livingstone, however, did not beat his African porters or servants. From the outset, he preferred to travel with relatively few porters and servants. An average European exploratory expedition would include well over 100 porters. Livingstone's porters were always numbered in the dozens, or less.

Livingstone began his first major exploration from South Africa in 1853. He had two objectives. First, he hoped to find a safe and reliable path for Europeans to follow into the center of the continent. Second,

TSETSE FLY

The tsetse fly is a small but formidable threat to humans and livestock in tropical Africa. The bloodsucking fly can transmit a parasite that causes "sleeping sickness" in both humans and livestock. Victims of this disease display fatigue and lethargy, which are commonly followed by death. Explorers in Africa in the eighteenth century found that European pack animals rarely survived for long in the tropical forests, and the explorers themselves suffered from lethargy while enduring the many illnesses that claimed so many lives. They attributed this lethargy to the tropical climate or malaria instead of to the bite of the tsetse fly. Europeans did, however, understand that their health was at greater risk in the tropical forests—the home of the tsetse fly—than in the grasslands or elevated plateaus, but the advantages of open or elevated terrain were again attributed to climate.

By the middle of the nineteenth century, Livingstone and other explorers were aware that the tsetse fly was a threat to livestock. However, they did not yet fully understand the nature of the threat. In the 1890s, David Bruce, an Australian surgeon in the British army, proved that the tsetse fly was transferring a parasite from wild animals to cattle. In 1901, physicians proved that "sleeping sickness" could be transferred from animals to humans.

he hoped to find a suitable place for a colonial settlement on the upper Zambezi River. He believed the land there would offer plentiful water and good prospects for agriculture. It also would be free of malaria (a deadly disease), the slave trade, and tsetse flies, which Livingstone knew to be a threat to livestock.

With a small group of servants and porters, Livingstone reached the mouth of the Zambezi River in May 1856. Livingstone became the first European to cross sub-Saharan Africa. More important, he had located what he believed to be an ideal location for a mission station and colonial settlement on the Batoka Plateau, near the upper Zambezi. He returned to fame and fortune in Great Britain, where he met Queen

Victoria, received a gold medal from the Royal Geographical Society, and published a best-selling book *Missionary Travels and Researches in South Africa.*

He returned to Africa in 1858 and led an expedition back up the Zambezi. He believed that he could reach the Batoka Plateau by boat. The expedition was a failure, but Livingstone's reputation was not ruined. In searching for a new objective, Livingstone turned to the greatest geographical mystery of his day: the source of the Nile River.

STANLEY'S EARLY LIFE

In 1841, in Denbigh, Wales, Henry Morton Stanley was born, like Livingstone, in poverty. His mother named him John Rowlands after his absent father. Rowlands took work as a deck hand on a ship bound from Liverpool for New Orleans. There, he met a wealthy merchant, Henry Morton Stanley. The merchant gave the grateful Rowlands his name as a token of his affection.

After the merchant died in 1861, the 20-year-old Stanley resumed a wayward existence under his new name. He fought for and deserted both the Confederacy and the Union in the U.S. Civil War. After the war's end, Stanley broke into journalism as a "special correspondent" for the *Missouri Democrat*, covering a U.S. government expedition to negotiate treaties with American Indian tribes. The *New York Herald* then hired Stanley to cover a British military expedition in Abyssinia (now Ethiopia), in East Africa. Impressed by his resourcefulness, the *Herald* next hired him to conduct one of the most remarkable publicity stunts in the history of newspapers. He was to search for Livingstone in central Africa.

STANLEY'S INSPIRATION

Knowing of Livingstone's fame as a missionary and explorer, Stanley worried that Livingstone might be critical of the motives behind his own expedition. Instead, Livingstone saw in Stanley's arrival a miracle. In Stanley's caravan he saw the means to resume his search for the head of the Nile. Livingstone observed of Stanley's caravan: "Bales of goods, baths of tin, huge kettles, cooking-pots, tents, etc., made me think, 'This must be a luxurious traveler, and not one at his wits' end like me." "I am not of a demonstrative turn," Livingstone stated, "but this disinterested kindness . . . so nobly carried into effect by Mr. Stanley, was simply overwhelming. I really do feel extremely grateful, and at the same time I am a little ashamed at not being more worthy of the generosity."

Livingstone recovered his strength within the week and gladly joined Stanley in conducting explorations of the northern shores of Lake Tanganyika. To Stanley's dismay, he could not persuade Livingstone to return with him to the coast. Livingstone was determined to resume his search for the source of the Nile. Stanley sent a large caravan of supplies back to Livingstone at Ujiji and then traveled home. His memoir, *How I Found Livingstone,* became an international best seller upon its publication in 1872. Stanley found himself transformed into an international celebrity, but he was far from satisfied. He was now intent upon joining the ranks of the great explorers and following Livingstone's call to bring "civilization" to Africa.

In addition to bringing back news that Livingstone was alive in Africa, Stanley also brought back Livingstone's papers to the British Foreign Office. These papers included his report on the massacre at Nyangwe. It sparked debates and expressions of moral outrage in the British Parliament, providing abolitionists with leverage to push for stronger measures against the slave trade. The government informed Said Burgash, the sultan of Zanzibar, that if he did not close his slave market, the Royal Navy would bombard the island. In June 1873 the sultan gave in, closing one of the oldest and busiest slave markets in Africa.

After Stanley's departure, Livingstone returned to his search for the source of the Nile. He had become convinced that the Lualaba River was part of the Nile itself. His theory flew in the face of facts. Most important, Livingstone might have taken measurements that would have demonstrated that the Lualaba River was lower than the lowest point known on the Nile River. Rivers do not, after all, flow uphill. However, Livingstone was not to be stopped as he set out to return to the Lualaba.

Although Livingstone's conviction and determination never failed him, his body eventually did. The explorer died of dysentery in May 1873. His African followers agreed that his body should be preserved and returned to his own people. This was an incredible undertaking that can only be explained by their loyalty to Livingstone. They removed the heart and internal organs from Livingstone's dead body

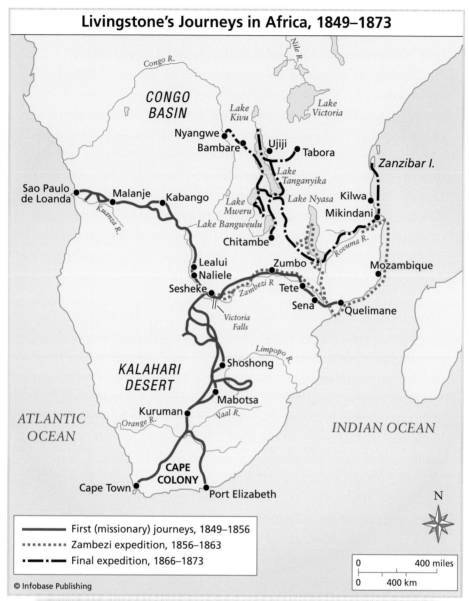

Livingstone's Journeys in Africa, 1849–1873

Legend:
— First (missionary) journeys, 1849–1856
••••••• Zambezi expedition, 1856–1863
—•—•— Final expedition, 1866–1873

0   400 miles
0   400 km

N

© Infobase Publishing

This map traces the three main journeys of David Livingstone. During his first expedition, he was one of the first Europeans to travel across Africa. On his second expedition, Livingstone carried out several official explorations in eastern and central Africa. His third and final expedition, where he searched for the source of the Nile, lasted until his death in 1873.

and buried these at the foot of a tree, into which they carved a simple memorial. This action was symbolic: The explorer's heart was buried in the heart of Africa. Livingstone's followers then carried his remains to the coast. There, British officials received the remains and shipped them to Britain.

In Britain, Livingstone's remains were welcomed as those of a hero. He was buried among kings and queens in a state funeral in Westminster Abbey in London. Stanley, the last white man to see Livingstone alive, helped carry the casket in the funeral. Then he went on to carry forward Livingstone's work in Africa. More than a century after Stanley's own death in 1904, he and Livingstone remain two of the most important figures in the modern age of exploration and empire.

2

The Modern Era of Exploration and Empire

BERNAL DÍAZ DEL CASTILLO WAS A FOOT SOLDIER IN THE SPANISH exploration and conquest of Mexico in the sixteenth century. He explained in his memoir his motives for joining in this risky adventure so far from home. He had desired "to serve God and His Majesty, to give light to those who were in darkness, and to grow rich, as all men desire to do." The light that Díaz desired to bring to Mexico was the word of the Christian God. Díaz believed that this God watched over the conquistadores and guided them in their explorations and in their many battles with the Aztec and other peoples of Central America. Many of the early European explorers agreed with Díaz. They believed that God had sanctioned their quest for riches under a divine plan to expand the borders of Christendom.

From the fifteenth to the twentieth centuries, Europeans explored in order to expand their empires. The objectives of European explorers changed, however, over this time frame. In the era of Bernal Díaz, European empires were largely identified by religious faith. They were ruled by kings and queens who sought gold and silver above all else. In the later years, European empires were largely identified by nationality. They were increasingly run by elected governments, or at least constitutional monarchs who sought raw materials and markets for their nation's industries.

A NEW WORLD FOR CHRISTIANS

In the fifteenth century, the kings and queens of Western Europe wanted to profit from the spice trade. *Spice* was a term that European merchants used to identify not only pepper and other spices but also silk, gem stones, and other luxury goods from Asia. The spice trade had been run overland for centuries along the fabled Silk Roads, such as the trade route between Damascus (present-day Syria) and Xian (present-day China). The Italians profited most from the spice trade, with merchant centers in Venice and Genoa and banking centers in Florence. This bothered the rulers of Spain, Portugal, France, and England. They wanted a share of the spice profits.

In an effort to thwart these Italian middle men, King Ferdinand and Queen Isabella of Spain hired Christopher Columbus to find a western sea route to Asia. Columbus was a ship captain from the Italian port city of Genoa. Columbus instead found the Caribbean, where, on October 12, 1492, he landed on an island that he named San Salvador. Columbus soon realized that he had not reached Asia. However, he believed that Asia was not far from this and other uncharted islands that he claimed for Spain.

At that time, Europeans believed that they knew of all the lands in the world. Everything they knew came from the histories of the Greeks and Romans and from the Bible. Yet, none of these texts had mentioned lands to the west of Europe and to the east of Asia, the so-called New World that Columbus and his crew encountered. Moreover, none of the texts had referred to the Arawak people, who Columbus met on San Salvador. They also did not mention any of the other peoples who Europeans would subsequently meet in the vast expanse of the Americas. Europeans were confused by the languages that these people spoke. They found the American cultures to be entirely unfamiliar. They looked for signs of what they regarded as "civilization." They looked for architecture like their own. They looked for farmlands, with fields ploughed and planted in straight lines. They looked for families organized like their own, but they could not perceive bonds of monogamous marriage between men and women. They looked for cities, but most peoples of the Americas did not have large urban centers. This was especially troubling to Europeans, who regarded the city as central to civilized society. (There were, in fact, some large cities in Central America.) Above all else, the European explorers were troubled to find that the peoples of this new world knew nothing of Christianity. Europeans debated whether these beings were humans at all.

Above, Christopher Columbus presents his plan to establish a direct trade route to India to the Spanish court of Queen Isabella and King Ferdinand. Initially, the project was rejected three times before the monarchs signed a contract with Columbus. He was granted 10 percent of the profits, noble status, and governship of the new territories to him and his descendants if he succeeded.

The prospects for conquest and conversion in the New World were apparent to Columbus. He wrote to Ferdinand and Isabella upon his return to Spain in 1493:

Since our Redeemer has given this victory to our most illustrious King and Queen, and to their famous realms, in so great a matter, for this all Christendom ought to feel joyful and make celebrations and give solemn thanks to the Holy Trinity with many solemn prayers for the great exaltation which it will have, in the turning of so many peoples to our holy faith, and afterwards for material benefits, since not only Spain but all Christians will hence have refreshment and profit.

The Catholic Church supported the Spanish monarchy in the exploration of the New World. This was important because at this time the pope held the authority to distribute any newly found lands under a principle called papal dominion. The Church's leader, Pope Alexander VI, decided which European countries would own lands in the New World. In 1493, the pope issued a formal declaration, called a bull, in which he drew an imaginary line across the map of the known world. The pope gave the lands on one side to Spain and the lands on the other side to Portugal. In effect, the pope gave Spain the New World. He gave Africa and the lands farther east to Portugal. The Spanish and Portuguese rulers agreed to this in the Treaty of Tordesillas in 1494.

This new era of European exploration was made possible not only by the pope but by naval technology. The great explorers benefited from relatively recent advances in navigation, such as the calculation of latitude from observation of the sun. They also benefited from advances in cartography, ship design, and shipborne artillery.

Access to these new technologies and financing for major voyages was then made possible by banks and financial networks that had supported the spice trade along the Silk Roads. Although Ferdinand and Isabella had attempted to avoid the Italian middle men of the spice trade, they inadvertently enabled Italian bankers to make even more money in overseas shipping to and from the Americas.

TO ASIA AND AROUND THE WORLD

As the conquistadores built a Spanish empire in Central and South America, the European powers continued their race to find a sea route to Asia. They circled the globe and established seaborne access to the coasts of Asia, Africa, and the Middle East—coasts from which

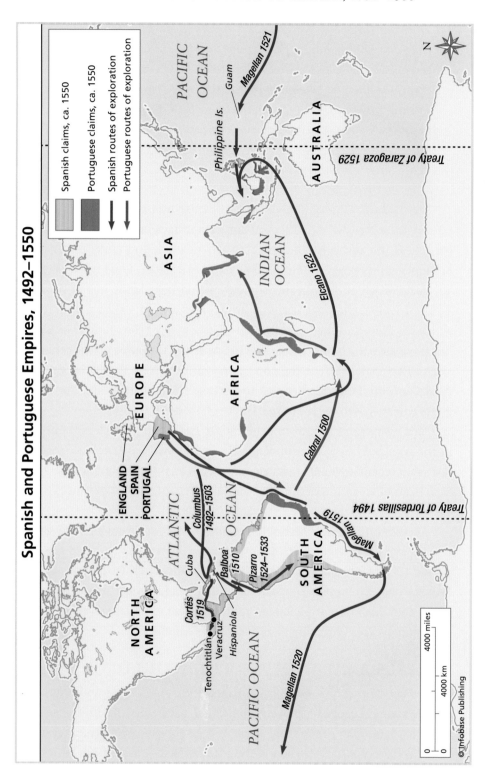

Spanish and Portuguese Empires, 1492–1550

Spanish claims, ca. 1550
Portuguese claims, ca. 1550
Spanish routes of exploration
Portuguese routes of exploration

PACIFIC OCEAN

Magellan 1521

Guam

Philippine Is.

AUSTRALIA

Treaty of Zaragoza 1529

ASIA

INDIAN OCEAN

Elcano 1522

EUROPE

AFRICA

Cabral 1500

ENGLAND
SPAIN
PORTUGAL

ATLANTIC OCEAN

Columbus 1492–1503

Cuba

Balboa 1510

Pizarro 1524–1533

Treaty of Tordesillas 1494

Magellan 1519

SOUTH AMERICA

Cortés 1519

Tenochtitlán
Veracruz
Hispaniola

NORTH AMERICA

PACIFIC OCEAN

Magellan 1520

N

4000 miles
4000 km

© Infobase Publishing

European explorers would proceed inland in the modern era. Another sailor from Genoa, John Cabot, approached the king of England, Henry VII. He explained that Columbus could not have reached islands off the coast of Asia. Cabot believed the distance to Asia simply had to be farther than Columbus had sailed. Cabot proposed, instead, to sail around the northern coast of the New World. In 1496, the king agreed to support this plan.

Cabot set sail, with his son Sebastian and 20 crewmen, from the port city of Bristol on the east coast of England in 1497. Cabot sailed beyond Ireland and reached North America, though scholars still debate where he exactly he landed. It is likely that he first went ashore on the coast of present-day Maine, then proceeded north to present-day Newfoundland. He explored the rocky coastline and saw signs of habitation, but he encountered no people. Cabot returned home.

King Henry hired Cabot once again to continue his search for a western route to Asia. Cabot set out once more in 1498, passed beyond Ireland and was never heard from again. The king sent Cabot's son Sebastian on a journey to seek the northern route to Asia. The younger Cabot also returned without success. After this attempt, the English Crown would not seriously return to the work of exploration until the rule of Queen Elizabeth, more than 60 years later.

John Cabot was the first of many European explorers to attempt to reach Asia via a northern passage around the New World. King Francis I of France sent Jacques Cartier on such a voyage in 1534. The king gave Cartier two ships and commissioned him "to discover certain islands and lands where it is said that a great quantity of gold, and other precious things, are to be found." The French monarch also persuaded Pope Clement VII to modify Pope Alexander VI's decision of 1493. Clement declared in 1533 that Pope Alexander's order applied only to lands that had been discovered already. It did not apply to lands that might be discovered in the future.

(opposite page) After Columbus returned from the New World, Spain and Portugal fought over territorial claims in the Americas. The empires saw the potential for great wealth from the newly discovered lands. In 1493, Pope Alexander VI issued a formal declaration, giving Spain control over the Americas and Portugal control over Africa and the lands farther east.

With the prospect of an overseas French empire before him, Cartier reached what is now Canada. He carefully mapped coastal regions and discovered the Gulf of St. Lawrence, which he claimed for his king. He also met an Iroquois chief, Donnaconna, and took two of the chief's sons back to the French court in 1534 as guests. These young men learned to speak French and went back with Cartier to Canada in 1535 as translators. In this second expedition the Iroquois led him to the St. Lawrence River, sailing up the river as far as present-day Montreal. This was Cartier's most important work as an explorer. The St. Lawrence would become the primary path that French colonists followed into the Canadian interior. After one final, relatively uneventful voyage, Cartier retired comfortably in France in 1542. Soon after, a new king who was not interested in exploration ruled France. Due to this and major religious wars within the country, French exploration would be suspended.

In contrast to the English and the French, the Portuguese attempted to reach Asia via a southern route around Africa. In the 1430s, Prince Henry the Navigator led Portuguese expeditions along the West African coast. Later, King John II of Portugal hired Bartholomeu Dias, a knight of the Portuguese court and a seaman with experience on the West African coast, to sail around the southern tip of Africa. Dias departed from Lisbon in August 1487 and rounded the southern tip of Africa in February 1488. He landed at what is now called Mossel Bay and encountered peoples called the Khoikhoi and the San. He then followed the coast eastward. He sailed as far as the Great Fish River, where his crew became fearful of the unknown waters. They persuaded Dias to turn back.

Dias returned to Lisbon after more than 17 months to great acclaim. He informed the king that on his return voyage he had seen a great cape at the bottom of Africa, which the king named the Cape of Good Hope. Dias had proven that it was possible to sail around Africa. However, he had also experienced the strong ocean currents that made a complete, round-trip voyage both difficult and dangerous. He would later captain one of three ships in the expedition of Pedro Alvarez Cabral. The ships left from Lisbon in 1500 and reached present-day Brazil for the first time. During the voyage from Brazil to the Cape of Good Hope, the expedition sailed into a terrible storm. Dias's vessel sank with all aboard.

The next king of Portugal, Manuel, was inspired by Columbus's discoveries. He pushed his captains to sail around the southern tip of Africa and on to Asia. He turned to Vasco da Gama, who had previously made a name for himself during naval combat against the French. Da Gama sailed from Lisbon with four ships and 170 men in July 1497. The ships rounded the Cape of Good Hope in November and landed in Mossel Bay. They traded with the Khoikhoi for cattle and other supplies. The expedition next made its way along the east coast of Africa. After reaching the port of Mozambique in March 1498, the Portuguese experienced problems with the Muslim leaders of several ports. Da Gama was relieved to find a friendly ruler at the port of Malinda. The ruler of Malinda even gave the Portuguese a guide who could help them across the Arabian Sea to Asia. Da Gama landed at Calicut, on the southwest coast of India, in May 1498. The Hindu raja welcomed them but would not sign a trade agreement. He feared upsetting Muslim traders in the port. Relations deteriorated when the raja refused either to receive da Gama's gifts or to trade because he felt da Gama's goods were cheap. After open hostilities and hostage taking, the raja agreed to trade with the Portuguese in the future. They must, however, bring him gold, silver, coral, and scarlet cloth. Satisfied, da Gama left.

During his voyage back to Portugal, half of da Gama's crew died from scurvy. Still, he reached Lisbon in September 1498 and was richly rewarded for his efforts. The king sent da Gama back to India in 1502 with orders to establish a Portuguese colony at Calicut. Da Gama succeeded by using horrific brutality. He died as the Portuguese viceroy to India, in the city of Cochin, in 1524.

The Portuguese now controlled the Cape of Good Hope. The Spanish king, Charles I (Holy Roman Emperor Charles V), also wanted to profit from the oceanic trade with Asia, so he hired Ferdinand Magellan to find a western sea route to Asia. With five ships and 560 men, Magellan set sail from Spain in September 1519. He took a southern course across the Atlantic and, after three months, reached the bay of what is now Rio de Janeiro in Brazil. Magellan then proceeded south, searching for a sea lane through South America. In March 1520, as the expedition sailed along the coast of present-day Argentina, the crews of three of the ships became frustrated with their seemingly hopeless search and mutinied. Magellan crushed the mutiny, killing two of his captains and

SCURVY

Scurvy is a disease that was a terrible threat to seamen until the nineteenth century. People get scurvy when they do not have enough vitamin C, resulting in the breakdown of the protein collagen. This is needed for connective tissue, bones, and healthy gums and teeth. One of the survivors of Magellan's voyage around the world, Pigafetta, wrote about the effects of scurvy among 30 of Magellan's men. "The gums of both the lower and upper teeth of some of our men swelled," Pigafetta recalled, "so that they could not eat under any circumstances." In addition to rotting gums and loss of teeth, scurvy produces swollen limbs and pain in one's joints. Scurvy afflicted every major overseas expedition until the eighteenth century, when Captain James Cook succeeded in preventing scurvy among his crew during his second voyage to the Pacific between 1772 and 1775. Although the symptoms of scurvy were well known, it would be centuries before scientists determined the source of the disease.

In the meantime, seamen and physicians fought scurvy by trial and error. They discovered that particular plants could prevent or cure scurvy but did not understand why. In the winter of 1535–1536, Cartier's men were dying of scurvy after their ship became frozen in the ice of the St. Lawrence River in Canada. They learned from local American Indians that they could cure themselves by drinking a concoction of boiled bark from a white cedar tree. Cartier's 85 men devoured the tree in a week. Cartier then brought home other specimens of the tree and planted them in the gardens of the French king.

In 1639, John Woodall wrote about "many excellent remedies" for scurvy. These included "Scurvy-grasse, Horse-Reddish roots, Nasturtia Aquatica, Wormwood, Sorrell, and many other good meanes." He also noted that in the Indies, seamen could obtain lemons, limes, and oranges, which were more effective against scurvy than anything found in England. In 1753, James Lind tested and confirmed that citrus fruits cured or prevented scurvy. In 1795, the British Royal Navy began to provide a daily ration of lime or lemon juice to its men. That is why the British are sometimes called "limeys" to this day.

leaving another stranded on the shore. The expedition then proceeded farther south. In October, Magellan's patience was rewarded. He sailed through a passage that opened into the Pacific Ocean—a passage now known as the Strait of Magellan.

Magellan then set out across the Pacific. His expedition had been reduced to three ships, due to the wreck of one vessel and the desertion of another. Scurvy was also taking a toll upon his remaining crew. Magellan did not know how far he would need to sail before reaching the nearest landfall. After months of hardship, in 1521 he succeeded in bringing his ships to the island now called Guam. There the ships were able to take on supplies. The expedition then proceeded to the islands now known as the Philippines, where Magellan was killed in a battle with the people of Mactan Island. The expedition continued, having little choice, and reached Asia in November. A single ship returned to Spain on September 8, 1522. It had only 17 crewmen aboard, the last survivors of Magellan's fleet.

THE EFFECTS OF EXPLORATION

European overseas exploration would contribute to significant developments within Europe itself. Spain gathered huge amounts of gold and silver from the New World and established itself as Europe's most powerful country in the sixteenth century. Exploration also enhanced European culture and the lives of common people. Although explorers and their crews were seldom men of high culture, their findings contributed to the Renaissance, a momentous era of intellectual and artistic achievement in Europe. Scholars read and wrote about explorations. For example, Thomas More, a scholar and influential figure in the English court of Henry VIII, read accounts of the Americas by Spaniards, Portuguese, and Italians. In 1516 he published an important book, *Utopia*, about a fictional, virtuous society. More placed it on a fictional island off the coast of the New World.

European exploration also brought new foods to Europe. In the sixteenth century, the population increased by about one-third, from approximately 80 million to 105 million. This population would feed itself in the coming decades with new foods imported from the Americas. The potato, for example, was brought from Peru to Spain in the 1530s. The potato was easily grown and offered high nutritional value.

It eventually became a staple in the diet of poor people in Spain and in other European countries, including Ireland.

For all their skill and courage, the European explorers brought terrible changes to the peoples in the Americas, Africa, and elsewhere. Due to the large number of deaths in the indigenous communities, and the ability of the peoples to flee the Europeans, the Portuguese began to bring slaves from Africa to Brazil in the 1550s. By the early seventeenth century, the English and the French copied the Spanish and Portuguese slave systems. They used slaves to grow sugar in the Caribbean. Later, slaves were forced to work on plantations in North America, where they grew tobacco, indigo, rice, and cotton.

The Europeans also desired to spread Christianity throughout the world. Catholicism came to dominate the religious landscape of much of the New World, but the road to this end was filled with conflict.

Finally, the European explorers brought with them new diseases. Both Europeans and African slaves brought with them influenza, yellow fever, bubonic plague, measles, whooping cough, malaria, and many other diseases against which the peoples of the New World had no immunity. The most deadly of these diseases was smallpox. Smallpox killed 50 to 100 percent of those infected. Within 50 years of the first contact with Europeans, the New World's indigenous population dropped from about 35 million to 15 million. This was due to deaths caused by disease. These diseases weakened the resistance of people who attempted to stop the Europeans' advance. Cortés, for example, benefited greatly from the ravages of European diseases within the Aztec Empire. As he attacked the capital city, Tenochtitlán, smallpox and other diseases had left people dying in the streets.

THE MODERN ERA OF EXPLORATION

Explorers in the modern era of empire—that period from about 1750 to 1950—commonly believed that their goals and methods differed from those of the conquistadores. The earlier era of exploration had been defined by remarkable feats of navigation. At the same time they had preached (or forced) conversion to Christianity, enslaved Native American peoples, then imported slaves from Africa when the Native Americans began to die in large numbers. By the mid-eighteenth century, explorers looked back critically upon the conquistadors and slave traders. They looked forward to serving the interests of commerce, science, and evangelical Christianity. The ideas behind exploration after the eighteenth century were products of their times. At the same time that there were important shifts in the imperial balance of power, there were huge developments in economics, science, religion, and nationalism. All of these combined to change the objectives and methods of exploration since the era of the conquistadores.

In the fifteenth and sixteenth centuries, Europe experienced an era of tremendous religious turmoil, known as the Reformation. The Reformation witnessed challenges to the practices and authority of the Catholic Church and the rise of new Christian denominations. In the early eighteenth century, the religious boundaries of Europe finally became stable. Wars were still fought between European powers, but these wars were not fought primarily over religion. Governments no longer depended on the pope to decide who owned new lands. They began to fight primarily over trade. Over the course of the 1600s, the imperial powers of Spain and Portugal regularly lost these wars over trade. Power shifted to the English, the French, and the Dutch. The British and French quadrupled their overseas trade in the eighteenth century. They replaced Spain and Portugal as Europe's greatest imperial powers.

After the eighteenth century, Europe's objectives in exploration were transformed by changing economies. In the sixteenth century, spices were most often luxury goods destined for the homes of the European elite. In the eighteenth century, European markets began to expand. Now goods were needed for the "middling ranks" of society, too. This group of people developed into what is now known as the "middle class." The middling ranks began to consume more and more goods from overseas. They wanted tea, sugar, porcelain, and cotton. European merchants placed greater emphasis on these goods and so, in turn, did explorers. From then on, European explorers would look beyond gold and silver to find other profitable commodities.

Europe's cities were growing. Goods were being produced in factories. Explorers began to look for raw materials needed to produce products like cocoa for chocolate candy and rubber for bicycle tires. They also began to look for new overseas markets for European goods. Finally, the explorers benefited from new technologies developed during this era. For example, they used steam engines to transport themselves up rivers. They used factory-produced rifles to defeat the indigenous people who opposed them.

Explorers in the modern age of empire were also influenced by science. New fields of study included botany (the study of plants), biology (the study of bodily processes of living organisms), archaeology (the study of the artifacts and other remains of peoples), and ethnology (the study of human cultures). Joseph Banks collected plant specimens in Tahiti. Alexander von Humboldt and A. J. A. Bonpland collected animal specimens on the upper Amazon River. John Lewis Burckhardt located the ancient city of Petra in Jordan.

The most significant scientific contribution to overseas exploration in the eighteenth century was the discovery of a method for determining longitude on the open ocean. Longitude is a system of measurement and location, pictured on maps as vertical lines passing between the north and south poles. In the fifteenth century, Europeans had learned how to determine latitude—another system of measurement and location represented on maps by horizontal lines. This allowed people to determine the distance traveled to the west or the east. Yet a method for measuring longitude had eluded Europeans, despite rich rewards offered by all of the major imperial powers. Finally, a clockmaker named John Harrison invented a clock, called a chronometer, that kept accurate time at sea. By the end of the eighteenth century, for the first time, an increasing number of ships' captains could determine both their latitude and longitude and thus their precise position on the open ocean.

JAMES COOK EXPLORES FOR SCIENCE

The modern era of European exploration began during the Enlightenment. Like the Renaissance before it, the Enlightenment was a period of important intellectual and artistic achievements. Enlightened thinkers employed scientific methods of objective, empirical investigation. The new significance of science and commerce are especially well illustrated by the modern voyages of Captain James Cook.

James Cook was born to Scottish farmers in 1728. He worked as a grocer's assistant before turning to the sea. He joined the British Royal Navy and quickly advanced through the ranks to become a warrant officer. After participating in Britain's victorious siege of the French at

Quebec, he was commissioned to survey the eastern coastline of Canada and the coasts of Newfoundland. In 1768, the Royal Society, a distinguished scientific body, cooperated with the Royal Navy to organize an expedition to the Pacific. This expedition had two purposes. First, the expedition was to witness the transit of Venus, when Venus passes between Earth and the sun. Scientists hoped observing this event would enable them to calculate the distance of the sun from Earth. The expedition had a secret mission, too. Cook was asked to determine whether there existed a Great Southern Continent somewhere in the Pacific. The expedition included a 25-year-old botanist named Joseph Banks. Banks brought a library, trunks full of scientific instruments, and a group of specialists, including artists.

Cook departed aboard the *Endeavour* in August 1768. He sailed around South America, searching unsuccessfully for the Southern Continent. He reached Tahiti in April 1769. Cook observed in his journal that his men should follow what he regarded as the first rule of trading:

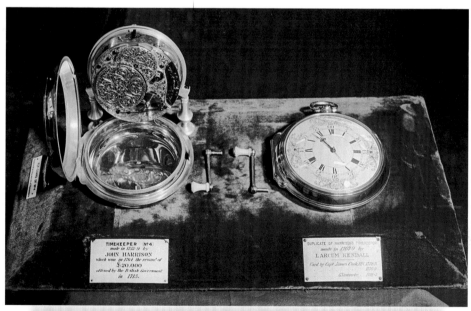

Before John Harrison invented the chronometer in 1730 (*shown above*), sailors were unable to measure the longitude of the place they visited in order to place it on a map. Harrison was able to produce a clock that could maintain accurate time on a lengthy voyage with varying conditions of temperature, pressure, and humidity.

"To endeavour by every fair means to cultivate a friendship with the Natives and to treat them with all imaginable humanity." Cook stayed in Tahiti for three months. He witnessed the transit of Venus, explored nearby islands, then proceeded to New Zealand and Australia before returning to England in July 1771.

EXPLORING FOR THE NATION

Exploration in the modern era was influenced by the rise of nationalism in Europe. The political phenomenon of nationalism had a number of sources. After the eighteenth century, the number of democratic governments grew. More and more people could read and write. The middle class was becoming increasingly important. In the nineteenth century, most explorers had a keen sense of national identity. Unlike in the sixteenth century, they worked on behalf of governments or businesses of their own nation. News of their achievements spread through the growing newspaper industry to a broader spectrum of society. The people of their own nation identified with them and basked in their reflected glory. The nation at large, rather than just the elite, supported exploration to a greater extent than ever before.

The power of exploration in building national pride was so great that it could even prompt nations to embrace foreign-born explorers as their own. Count Pietro di Brazza Savorgnani was an Italian aristocrat who, as a young man, joined the French navy and became a French citizen. He undertook explorations in Africa on behalf of his adopted country. The French criticized his Italian accent, until he upstaged the great explorer Henry Morton Stanley in establishing France's claim to territory on the Congo River. The Italian-born Brazza became the toast of Paris. He was hailed until his death as a national treasure.

APPROACHES TO SAVAGERY

At the outset of the modern era of empire, explorers were drawn to three regions of the world: Central Asia, Africa, and the Middle East. Explorers sought to advance the strategic interests of their governments. They sought to find raw materials and new markets for European industries. They also sought to spread Christianity, along with commercial development. Finally, and undoubtedly, most explorers also sought adventure.

Europeans pursued many different objectives in their explorations and brought with them many different ideas about the foreign peoples who they encountered. There were some who believed that Europeans should respect differences between cultures, build commercial relationships, and learn from other peoples. In Denis Diderot's *Dialogue between A and B*, the Tahitian, Orou, observes: "You would not judge European morals by those of Tahiti, so do not judge Tahitian ones by yours." There were also explorers who firmly believed that they could both respect foreign peoples and improve their lives by changing not only their religious beliefs but also their cultures and economies.

The majority of explorers took a less respectful view of the peoples they encountered. In 1860 Sir Francis Galton, an English scientist, published *The Art of Travel*. This book became a standard reference guide for explorers. He played down the risks of travel, noting with an encouraging tone that young men died in smaller proportions than older men. For those who encountered "natives," Galton advised: "A frank, joking, but determined manner, joined with an air of showing more confidence in the good faith of the natives than you really feel, is the best." He continued:

> *If a savage does mischief, look on him as you would on a kicking mule, or a wild animal, whose nature is to be unruly and vicious, and keep your temper quite unruffled. Evade the mischief, if you can: if you cannot, endure it; and do not trouble yourself over-much about your dignity, or about retaliating on the man, except it be on the grounds of expediency.*

Despite Galton's poor attitude toward "native" peoples, he was nonetheless an explorer of the modern era and not a conquistador. Galton reminded his reader to bear in mind the common humanity of the "civilized" person and the "savage." "Savages rarely murder newcomers," Galton assured the would-be explorer. "They fear their guns, and have a superstitious awe of the white man's power: They require time to discover that he is not very different to themselves."

3

The Great Game in Central Asia

Lieutenant Francis Younghusband, a young British officer in the Army of India, dismounted from his camel. It was July 23, 1887, and he was on a journey from Peking (Beijing), China, to India. He and a guide, a Mongol assistant, a Chinese personal servant, and eight camels had covered 1,200 miles (1,931 kilometers) of desert in three months. With what he described as "unspeakable relief," Younghusband now entered Hami, a small trading town on the western edge of the Gobi Desert in Central Asia. It was a crossroads for Central and East Asian peoples, including Turks, Kalmaks, Mongols, Chinese, and others. The town lay on the easternmost border of Turkestan. The Chinese had taken over this land earlier in the century. It was not, however, the Chinese Empire that Younghusband was interested in. He was looking for information about the Russian Empire, which was steadily expanding southward toward India, the so-called jewel in Britain's imperial crown.

This was the era of the Great Game, a term used by Rudyard Kipling in his book *Kim*. The game was no friendly contest but an intense, often violent competition for dominance. The Great Game was played on the vast field of Central Asia. This is a region of great geographical diversity, distinguished by its combination of numerous deserts and mountain ranges. It is crucial to the life of South and East Asia because it is the source of all of Asia's major rivers and because it is the hub of ancient overland trade routes.

In the early nineteenth century, the Russian Empire had begun to expand, causing concern among British officials in India. They set about fortifying India's northern borders against a Russian advance into Afghanistan, the kingdom of Kashmir, or the kingdoms of Nepal and Tibet. Russia's growth was not fast, but it was steady. Younghusband

Russian and British Empires in Asia, 1822–1914

Russia's steady expansion into Central Asia threatened Great Britain's control over the Indian subcontinent. This rivalry between the two great powers, also called the Great Game, came to an end when Russia and Great Britain agreed to make a stand against the German advance in the Middle East.

described it as being like a glacier. In anticipation of the Russian glacier's progress, he arrived in Hami and began looking for an officer who was supposed to meet him there.

Colonel Mark Bell was the director of military intelligence of the Army of India. Bell needed Younghusband to help him learn about the Chinese Turkestan army's defenses. He was worried that if the Russians took over Turkestan they could easily reach northern India through the Himalayas. If Bell and Younghusband found that Chinese Turkestan was not sufficiently fortified, then the British would have to increase their defenses. Bell and Younghusband took separate routes. Although they had intended to meet at Hami, their paths never crossed. In the end, they both reached India. Their achievement had not only military, but also exploratory significance. They became the first Europeans to travel from Peking to India through Central Asia.

In the nineteenth and twentieth centuries, European explorations in Central Asia received far less attention than did those in Africa. Younghusband wrote in 1937, "Fifty years ago it was thought that Africa was the only field for what might truly be termed exploration. It was taken for granted that all that was worth knowing about Asia was already known." As Younghusband was aware, this could not have been farther from the truth. "At any rate," he stated of his journey from Peking to India, "I found new ways across the greatest desert in the world and over the highest mountains; and my journey on foot, on camels, and on ponies, was in extent farther than from New York to San Francisco and led across a range twice as high as the Rocky Mountains." Such explorations were part of a greater game of European competition around the world.

COOPERATION AND CONFLICT BETWEEN BRITAIN AND RUSSIA IN ASIA

Competition between Britain and Russia in Central Asia was slow to develop. For centuries, Britain was far more interested in breaking into the lucrative sea trade with Southeast Asia, India, and China. Toward this end, a group of London merchants pooled their money. They founded the East India Company (EIC) in 1600. It competed primarily with Dutch, Portuguese, and French merchants. In the mid-1700s, the

EIC in India seized some of the powers of India's Mughal emperor and became involved not only in trade but also in tax collection. After the late eighteenth century, the EIC extended its control on the Asian subcontinent, not just as a commercial firm. It was also a government. The British in India began to look northward toward Central Asia.

The Russians made their own approach to Central Asia by land rather than by sea. Before turning to Central Asia, however, they established their dominance over Siberia, the vast region to the north of what would become the Great Game. By the early nineteenth century, Russia had established its power over much of the lands eastward from the Ural Mountains to the Arctic and Pacific oceans. The Russians and the British found themselves moving simultaneously toward Central Asia from the north and south, respectively.

Russian forces advanced southward into the Caucasus, the region west of the Caspian Sea, toward northern Persia. The Russians took over the Caucasus and then looked eastward. Their next prize was beyond the Caspian Sea, a collection of Muslim khanates, including Khiva and Bukhara. The Great Game opened with two Russian diplomatic missions to these kingdoms.

The first Russian participant in the Great Game was Captain Nikolai Muraviev. He reached Khiva in 1819 disguised as a member of the Turkmen tribe, in the midst of a merchant caravan. Muhammad Rahim, the khan of Khiva, had warned the Russians to stay away from his kingdom. He was angered that no one had bothered to kill Muraviev before he reached the capital. However, because he was afraid of the Russians, the khan negotiated an alliance with Muraviev. In 1820 the Russians sent a diplomatic mission to Bukhara with the intention of opening commercial relations. Although the Russians were kept outside the gates of the city, a German member of the mission snuck into the capital in disguise and collected information for three months. Like the khan of Khiva, Haidar, the emir of Bukhara, negotiated with the Russians. He, too, feared them.

At the beginning of the nineteenth century, the Russian and British Empires in Central Asia were separated by about 2,000 miles (3,218 km). By the end of the century, they were as close as 20 miles (32 km) apart. Exploration was essential to the rapid, and potentially volatile, expansion of these empires in the era of the Great Game.

LOOKING FOR THE FINEST HORSES IN THE WORLD

The first of the British explorers in the Great Game was neither a soldier, nor a diplomat. He was not even a geographer by training. He was, instead, a distinguished veterinarian named William Moorcroft. Moorcroft specialized in the treatment of lame horses. The EIC hired Moorcroft in the early years of the nineteenth century to assist in locating breeding stock for its cavalry. He was already in his forties, but he was about to begin an entirely new life.

One might have expected Moorcroft to begin his travels in Central Asia in search of horses. Instead, he set out in 1812 in search of goats, a sacred lake, and, perhaps, Russians. Why goats? Moorcroft was impressed by the Indian shawl industry. The fine woolen shawls of India were sold to Europe at considerable profit. It had occurred to Moorcroft that if one could breed Indian goats in Britain, then one could make the same shawls in greater numbers using factories and become rich. Moorcroft found a partner in Hyder Young Hearsey. The two men then hired an Indian who understood the languages, cultures, and negotiating techniques that they might encounter in their travels. Their plan was to cross the central Himalayas and purchase goats. In the end they would also answer long-standing questions about the river systems of South Asia.

Moorcroft and Hearsey set off for the Niti Pass through the central Himalayas. They were disguised as Hindu merchant pilgrims on their way to the sacred lake of Manasarowar. They traveled in disguise in order to avoid the Nepalese soldiers, known as Gurkhas, who patrolled the Himalayas. The Nepalese rulers were on bad terms with the EIC and deeply suspicious of European travelers in their realm. The small expedition successfully made it through the pass and arrived on the Tibetan plateau. They made their way across the plateau, acquiring goats as Moorcroft mapped the land. He established the positions of a couple of major lakes and located the upper reaches of the Indus and Sutlej Rivers. To Hearsey's amusement, Moorcroft was constantly pausing to examine flowers, lizards, rocks, yaks, and anything else that struck him as unfamiliar. He kept detailed records of his observations. On one occasion, he was surprised to see two European dogs, a pug and a terrier. Moorcroft learned that they had been purchased from

Disguised as Hindu trading pilgrims, William Moorcroft and Hyder Young Hearsey set out in search of Tibetan goats. These goats provided fine wool, which was then crafted into beautiful shawls and sold at considerable profit. Pictured is a Kashmir shawl from the nineteenth century.

Russians. He saw these dogs as clear evidence of the Russian threat in the Himalayas. He described this threat in one of his many reports to the government of India.

The pilgrims proceeded to Lake Manasarowar, which was and is very difficult to reach at 15,000 feet (4,572 meters). Not only was the lake sacred to many Asian faiths, it was also widely believed to be the source of the Ganges River in India. Indian and European geographers alike also believed the lake to be the source of the Indus, the Sutlej, and the Tsangpo rivers. Moorcroft walked much of the way around the lake and sent his servants to examine the remaining shores that he could not see.

They found no outlets. Moorcroft concluded that this sacred lake was not, in fact, the source of the Ganges or any of Asia's other major rivers.

News of Moorcroft and Hearsey eventually reached the Nepalese capital of Kathmandu. The raja promptly sent Gurkhas to capture the men. The expedition made its way home in October, accompanied by a herd of goats. It was followed by a growing number of Gurkha troops. The Gurkhas finally captured Moorcroft, Hearsey, and their men just 50 miles (80 km) from the British frontier. Remarkably, Moorcroft was able to smuggle out a letter to his superiors. This letter reached the British government in Calcutta. The governor-general made a personal appeal to the raja of Nepal for the release of the men. In just 17 days, the men were freed.

Moorcroft's expedition had mixed results. On the one hand, geographers and British officials were delighted to acquire Moorcroft's geographical information about the Himalayas, particularly its lakes, snowmelts, and rivers. On the other hand, such information would be even harder to get in the future because western Tibet was closed to Europeans after Moorcroft and Hearsey's travels. As for the goats, they were shipped off to Scotland. Many died in the foreign environment, and those that survived produced wool of only average quality.

In 1819, at age 52, Moorcroft undertook his next expedition to the northwest. The EIC sent Moorcroft to buy horses in Bukhara. There were rumors that excellent horses from Afghanistan could be found there. This would certainly have been no small undertaking, as a mission of this nature required a large amount of supplies, money, gifts, and an armed escort. Moorcroft assembled a large caravan consisting of more than eight tons of supplies, which were carried, at one point, by six elephants and forty camels. In contrast to his previous travels in disguise, Moorcroft now looked every bit the British official. He brought his own large tent, complete with carpets, folding chairs, and a mahogany writing desk.

Along the way, Moorcroft applied to the Chinese government for permission to proceed into Turkestan. He waited two years for a reply. In the meantime, he occupied himself with mapping. His work contributed significantly to the EIC's geographical knowledge of the region. After the Chinese rejected his application to cross into Turkestan, he proceeded to Kashmir in 1822 and examined the manufacture of woolen shawls. He then traveled to Kabul in Afghanistan, where he reported that Russians were spying on him. Over these first several years of his travels, Moorcroft acquired a tremendous amount of information. However, he did little in the way of purchasing horses. So in 1824, the EIC asked him to return. Moorcroft found excuses to ignore this order, and after some five years, in February 1825, he finally arrived in Bukhara.

Much to his dismay, he could not find horses of outstanding quality for sale in Bukhara. Moorcroft did, however, find evidence of growing Russian influence in the kingdom. He set up a spy network, and over five months he investigated everything from Russians to winemaking to intestinal parasites.

From Bukhara, Moorcroft set out once more to find the horses of Turkestan, which he regarded as "the finest horses in the world." He was told that these horses were with the emir, who was attacking an enemy of his kingdom. When Moorcroft caught up with the emir's army, he found the excellent stallions he had sought for more than five years. The emir initially approved the sale. Then, suddenly, he put a stop to it and ordered Moorcroft to depart. Greatly disappointed, Moorcroft set off for home, crossing the desert to the Oxus River in August. After that, his fate is unknown. It is possible that Moorcroft died of fever while still searching for horses. Moorcroft's many notes, reports, and personal papers were discovered throughout Central Asia in the years to come. They provided the British with unprecedented knowledge of the geographies and cultures of the region.

EXPLORER SPIES

The British and the Russians found it increasingly difficult to conduct explorations themselves. There were two problems. First, as Europeans, they were easily found by hostile regimes, as in the case of Moorcroft and Hearsey in Nepal. Second, their enemies could easily keep track of their explorations for their own benefit. Both nations solved these problems by having the indigenous peoples explore for them. The British relied on Indians. The Russians came to rely on Buddhists from Mongolia for access to Tibet.

In the 1860s, the newly founded Government of India began to train Indians as spies. They wanted to gain access to Tibet and Chinese Turkestan to gather geographical information. These spies were commonly known as pundits, a term for guides knowledgeable in local culture and geography. The first of these spies was a Muslim named Mohamed-i-Hameed. He traveled under cover to Yarkand in Turkestan and stayed for six months. He took notes on geography and

TOOLS FOR SURVEYING

The Indian pundits who collected geographical information in the Great Game were trained at the offices of the Survey of India in Dehra Dun. Here they were shown how to use both conventional and unconventional tools of mapping. Surveyors in the nineteenth century generally used five basic tools. The first tool, used in measuring distance, was a 66-foot-long chain. Each surveyor also carried a compass, used to figure out the direction of a line. The surveyor then used either or both of two tools, a transit and a theodolite, held by a tripod. These measured angles. Finally, the surveyor used a level to measure elevations.

The Indian pundits engaged in the Great Game were trained in more discreet methods of gathering information. They were given specially made tools that were much smaller than normal size. These tools were then concealed in boxes with hidden compartments. They also used tools more familiar to explorers than surveyors. For example, the pundits took "boiling point" readings of altitude with a thermometer, knowing that water boils at different temperatures, depending on one's position above sea level. They could not extend a 66-foot chain to measure distances, so they trained themselves to take steps of regular length. They then kept track of these steps by counting their paces on the Tibetan rosaries that they carried.

Perhaps most ingenious of all was their adaptation of the Tibetan prayer wheel for their purposes. The most common prayer wheel is small enough to be held in one's hand. It consists of a cylinder that rotates atop a handle made of copper or silver. Inside the cylinder are scrolls of paper on which is written the most important Tibetan prayer. When the pundits traveled in disguise as Tibetans, they replaced the prayer scrolls with their geographical notes.

Russian activities in the region. He died of an unknown illness during his return journey, but his notes were recovered and found to be filled with valuable information. The British then recruited two Tibetan-speaking Indians who lived in the Himalayan foothills to spy in Tibet. These men, Nain Singh and Mani Singh, were trained for two years in surveying in secrecy. For example, they were trained to count their steps in order to measure distances.

The two men attempted to travel via Nepal to Tibet, but only one man, Nain Singh, reached Lhasa in Tibet after a year. He figured out the precise latitude and altitude of the capital for the first time. He also collected general information, and even attended an audience with the Dalai Lama. He returned to India after one and a half years and produced an entirely new map of Tibet. Later, he visited the Thok Jalung goldfields of western Tibet, located at an altitude of over 16,000 feet (4,876 m). For his years of service, Nain Singh won the gold medal of the Royal Geographical Society.

As the British devoted greater resources to training Indians in the arts of surveying and spying, the Russians still relied upon military officers to conduct their explorations. The most successful Russian explorer of Central Asia of the time was Colonel Nikolai Prejevalsky. Over 17 years he led six expeditions, locating many important geographical sites, including the source of the Yellow River. Although Prejevalsky was a military officer, he was keenly interested in science. He gathered information on everything from geology to wild camels, and he brought back many specimens, including hundreds of pressed flowers.

In 1867, Prejevalsky became the first European to cross the Gobi Desert in Chinese Turkestan. In 1877, he returned to Turkestan and followed the Tarim River to Lake Lob Nor. This lake had not been seen by a European since Marco Polo in the thirteenth century. From Lob Nor he went south to become the first European to explore the Atyn Dagh Mountains, all the while under the watchful eye of Chinese officials who were unhappy about his presence in their land.

RACING FOR A FORBIDDEN CITY

The biggest prize in the Great Game was the capital of Tibet—Lhasa. Lhasa is found at an elevation of 12,000 feet (3,657 m), making it the highest capital in the world. It is surrounded by mountains, and the only way to reach the city was through dangerous mountain passes that were closed by snow for much of the year. Travelers experienced subzero temperatures, blinding snow, and strong winds that could knock a rider off his or her horse. Despite the harsh climate, the people of Tibet developed a rich culture based on the religion of Buddhism. This religion had developed for more than a thousand years from the teachings of Siddhartha Gautama.

When Europeans began to arrive in Tibet after the eighteenth century, they found the country ruled by a Dalai Lama, a Buddhist monk with both spiritual and political power. Dalai Lamas oversaw more than 2,000 monasteries that were made up of about one of every six Tibetan men. At least one boy from every family became a monk. In the years of the Great Game, Tibet was part of China. However, Chinese power in the region had been slipping away for decades.

The first Europeans to reach Lhasa in the modern era—and then survive to document their visit—were two French Catholic priests, Father Huc and Father Gabet. These priests had been working as missionaries among the Buddhists of Mongolia. They had hoped to convert the leading Buddhist monks of Tibet and, especially, the Dalai Lama. The priests departed from Mongolia in 1844, approaching Lhasa from the northeast. The climate in this region was bitterly cold. After breakfast, they would mix barley meal, called tsamba, and tea into a paste. They would press this paste into balls to eat later. They would place the balls of boiling hot paste in a cloth and put this against the skin of their chests. Over this each man wore a sheepskin vest, a lambskin waistcoat, a fox fur coat, and a woolen robe. "Every day of that fortnight," says Huc, "our tsamba-cakes froze; when we took them out they were like solid putty, yet they had to be eaten, at the risk of breaking one's teeth, to avoid perishing of hunger."

In this frozen wasteland, the men and animals began to die. The camels could not maintain their footing on ice. At times, the men had to use knives and axes to cut the ice ahead of the camels so that their soft feet could take hold. When the camels fell, they commonly refused to get up. Their loads would simply be transferred onto the surviving animals before the caravan moved on. The caravan also left behind 40 men who died from the cold. Huc observes, "When we had all passed by, the crows and the vultures which ceaselessly wheeled above us swooped down on these wretches, who no doubt had enough life left in them to feel the talons that tore them." Father Gabet was nearly killed by the cold, but Father Huc refused to abandon him and tied him to one of their camels. Gabet miraculously recovered as the caravan began its ascent of the mountains. There they lost more animals and men as they crossed icy rivers and made their way through the dangerous passes to Lhasa.

After climbing the final mountain, the caravan began its descent into Lhasa, which Huc describes:

> *The sun was just about to set when we had negotiated all the zig-zags of the descent. We came out into a wide valley, and on our right we saw Lhasa, capital of the Buddhist world. A multitude of ancient trees; large white houses, flat-roofed and turreted; countless temples with golden roofs; the Buddha La, with the palace of the Dalai Lama on it: all this we saw, an impressive and majestic city.*

The French priests entered Lhasa in January 1846. Their plans to convert Buddhists into Christians never worked out. Instead, they were arrested, and government officials arranged to have them escorted out of the country. Fathers Huc and Gabet were lucky not to pay for their visit to Lhasa with their heads. Another European would not enter Lhasa until Francis Younghusband in 1904. Lhasa became known as a "forbidden city." This made it all the more attractive to European explorers.

THE GREAT GAME WON

Francis Younghusband had already distinguished himself as an explorer when he became one of the first two Europeans to travel from Peking to India in 1887. He had crossed the Gobi Desert and had led important explorations of Turkestan. Before reaching India, Younghusband was also the first European to cross the Himalayas through the Mustagh Pass. Sixteen years later, he was also a well-respected and well-connected member of the Government of India. The viceroy (governor), Lord Curzon, had long feared a Russian threat from the Himalayas. When he became convinced that India's defense depended on immediate action, he turned to Younghusband. Younghusband was asked to go to Tibet to impose British control.

A century before, the British might have thought twice about taking this action. They would have feared war with China. Now, however, China had lost all power in Tibet, although it maintained a political representative at Lhasa. Britain had only Russia to fear. Lord Curzon decided to take action. He sent Younghusband into Tibet with an army, complete with artillery, in 1904. They fought Tibetan soldiers with terrible results. On one occasion, the British soldiers stopped shooting the Tibetan troops without orders to do so because they found the slaughter to be inhumane.

Following the collapse of Tibetan resistance, Younghusband led his forces to Lhasa. He became the first European to enter the city in almost 60 years. He did not find the Dalai Lama, who had fled into a temporary exile. He also did not find evidence of Russian influence. In September 1904, he signed the Anglo-Tibetan Convention with the Dalai Lama's regent, who had remained behind with the Dalai Lama's official seal. This convention opened Tibet to British trade, stopped the Tibetans from dealing with other powers without British approval, and provided for a British occupation force until the Tibetan government paid the cost of Younghusband's expedition.

So the British claimed the most coveted prize in the Great Game. However, it was events outside Central Asia that ended the game. After the late nineteenth century, Germany became an enemy of both Britain and Russia. The two nations became uneasy allies. Also, within 13 years of the Anglo-Tibetan Convention, the czarist regime in Russia was overthrown. The new Russian government did not care about boundary lines in Central Asia.

Even after the Great Game, important explorations in Central Asia would continue. Younghusband's own work was far from finished. He would return to the Himalayas and support the exploration of the top of the world, the peak of Mount Everest.

Imperial rivalries had driven European explorations in Central Asia over the course of the nineteenth century. These explorations had been followed by Europe's political dominance over the region. However, the daily lives of the peoples of Central Asia were, for the most part, not changed. European Christian missionaries failed to

In order to prevent Russia from gaining control of Tibet, which would provide a direct route to British India, Great Britain sent Colonel Francis Younghusband to its capital to lead a large military mission. The bloody battle ended with the British occupation of Lhasa. Above, Younghusband's troops fall on a steep mountain pass during their expedition to Tibet.

convert most of the Muslims, Buddhists, and Hindus of the region. Likewise, European commerce was slow to expand in Central Asia. The region was largely untouched by industrial development for many decades. The harsh climate and geography stopped Russians from settling in many areas.

As Europeans continued their explorations well into the 1920s and 1930s, they commonly met people who had never even seen a watch. These people went about their lives much as their great-grandparents had done, unaware of many scientific and technological developments that had transformed Western society over the previous 200 years. This situation would begin to change throughout much of Central Asia only after the 1930s and 1940s, when the communist regimes of the Soviet Union and China introduced progressive programs.

4

Following the Niger and the Nile

THE MODERN ERA OF EUROPEAN EXPLORATION OF THE GREAT rivers of Africa began in a London tavern. In June 1788, Sir Joseph Banks, formerly the chief scientist on Captain Cook's first expedition to the Pacific and now the president of the Royal Society, was having dinner with some influential friends. These 12 men shared many interests in science, and especially geography. They were prepared to use their own wealth for exploration. They agreed to the following resolution:

> *That, as no species of information is more ardently desired, or more generally useful, than that which improves the science of Geography; and as the vast Continent of Africa, notwithstanding the efforts of the Ancients, and the wishes of the Moderns, is still in a great measure unexplored, the members of this Club do form themselves into an Association for Promoting the Discovery of the Inland Parts of that Quarter of the world.*

They founded the Association for Promoting the Discovery of the Interior Parts of Africa. They knew that rivers provided a way of traveling into the African interior and chose the exploration of the Niger River as their first goal. Europeans knew that the Niger was important, however, they did not know where it ended. By contrast, the mystery of the Nile River in the northeast of Africa lay not in its end, but in its beginning. In 1831, the Association for Promoting the Discovery of the Interior Parts of Africa became part of the Geographical Society of London. This organization eventually would be renamed the Royal Geographical Society. It made the discovery of the source of the Nile the greatest geographical cause of the nineteenth century.

Europeans had a variety of motives for attempting to track these two great rivers. They wanted to evaluate commercial prospects in the African interior. Others desired to expose and combat the African slave trade or to spread the Christian faith. After the slave trade was abolished in 1807 and slaves were emancipated in the British Empire in 1833, explorers intended to replace the slave trade with "legitimate commerce" between Africans and Europeans.

FINDING THE NIGER

The Niger River flows for 2,600 miles (4,184 km). It is one of the longest rivers in the world. It is the only major river in Africa that begins by flowing away from the ocean. That is one reason why European explorers had so much trouble determining its course. In addition to the unusual starting point of the Niger, several other factors made the river difficult for Europeans to find. While the desolate terrain of the Sahara Desert, the terrible heat, and the animosity of Muslims to exploration by Christians complicated the northern approach to the river, the West African coast harbored diseases that killed Europeans at alarming rates. It prompted Europeans to refer to the region as the "white man's grave." Finally, the mouth of the Niger is not obvious, because it takes the form of a delta with numerous outlets to the ocean. For more than 2,000 years Europeans had wondered about the course of the Niger and where it met the sea.

With virtually no accurate information available, the Association for Promoting the Discovery of the Interior Parts of Africa decided that it should approach the Niger from the northeast. The initial attempt was not, however, promising. The association's first explorer, an American named John Ledyard, reached Cairo and then died of a "bilious complaint." A second explorer had traveled as far as Libya and then turned back. A third explorer, Daniel Houghton, made it into the interior from the west, then was robbed and murdered by Muslim merchants.

Joseph Banks turned to Mungo Park, a Scottish doctor with an interest in botany. In 1796, the association instructed Park to follow

The Royal Geographical Society was founded in 1831. It started as a dining club, where members held debates on scientific issues of its time. This engraving shows an 1859 reception at the society for the English explorer John Hanning Speke.

Houghton's path to the Niger. Traveling through the lands of the Mandingo, Foulah, and Bambarran, he underwent numerous hardships, including fever, robbery, and imprisonment. Finally, a caravan of Kaartans, members of a tribe who were fleeing local wars, brought him to the Niger and then to Segu, the capital of Bambarra. Park found that the Niger flowed *eastward*. Park asked the king of Segu for assistance across the river to the king's home, but the king was worried that if he received this Christian traveler, he might offend his Muslim subjects.

After receiving shelter from a kind African woman, Park continued eastward to Silla, where he finally decided to turn back. Before traveling west, he attempted to learn all that he could about the lands downriver. Park turned westward in August and traveled through heavy rains.

After leaving the river, Park was again robbed. They stripped him naked but before they left, they tossed him a shirt, his trousers, and his hat. The hat contained his notes stuck inside the crown. "After they were gone," Park recalls, "I sat for some time, looking around me with amazement and terror . . . I saw myself in the midst of a vast wilderness, in the depth of the rainy season; naked and alone; surrounded by savage animals, and men still more savage. I was five hundred miles from the nearest European settlement."

Park made his way to the town of Sibidooloo. To Park's great surprise, the chief received him with kindness and returned his belongings, enabling him to continue his journey. Park joined a slave caravan for both protection and guidance to the coast. Park caught a slave ship to Antigua in the Caribbean, from which he returned to Britain. His report that the Niger flows eastward rather than westward settled a major issue of African geography.

The British government sent Park back to the Niger in 1805 to follow the river to its end. This time, Park was supported by a large expedition. By June, so many of his men were dying from fever and dysentery that he no longer stopped to bury them, nor did he wait for the sick who could no longer keep up. The last of his men reached the Niger on August 19. After building a vessel to sail down the Niger, the precise circumstances of the deaths of Park and his men remain mysterious. It appears probable that the expedition ended in an ambush just 600 miles (956 km) from the mouth of the river.

SPEKE FINDS THE SOURCE OF THE NILE

The Nile River flows more than 4,000 miles (6,437 km) northward from central Africa to the Mediterranean Sea. Europeans had been aware of the river for thousands of years because it lay near important trade routes and the great empires of ancient Egypt that grew up along its banks. Europeans did not know where the river began. Historians and geographers had long believed that it must flow from a massive, inland lake.

In the 1770s, a Scot named James Bruce traveled to Abyssinia in northeast Africa in order to locate the source of the Nile. Instead, he spent three eventful years in the court of Tekle Haimanot II, the emperor of Abyssinia. He found the source of the so-called Blue Nile, a major tributary of the larger river, known as the White Nile.

Europeans found tremendous strategic importance in the Nile when the French armies of Napoleon Bonaparte invaded Egypt in 1798. Napoleon's arrival in Egypt sent a message to both the British and Russian

MALARIA AND QUININE

Malaria is a disease caused by a blood parasite passed on to humans by the bite of certain kinds of mosquitoes. In the eighteenth and nineteenth centuries, Europeans generally referred to malaria as "fever." The symptoms ranged from debilitating weakness and aching limbs to intense headaches, loss of appetite, and delirium. Malaria can result in death, as it commonly did among Europeans in Africa until the mid-nineteenth century.

Although almost all European explorers in Africa endured bouts of fever, few could agree on its cause. The most common explanation was that "miasmas" from swamps produced fever. Some believed that it was caused by strenuous activity in damp clothing, while others believed that it was carried in rain. David Livingstone was the only major explorer to propose that fever was somehow caused by mosquitoes. Given the variety of possible causes of fever, there were many possible cures, virtually all of which did not work. Some doctors recommended a cold bath, while others recommended swallowing arsenic. In fact, Europeans had been aware of an effective cure for fever since the sixteenth century, when the indigenous peoples of Peru informed Jesuit missionaries that fever could be cured by drinking an infusion made with the bark of the Cinchona tree. Still, no one understood what it was about the bark that made it effective in combating fever. In the nineteenth century, two French pharmacists answered this question by isolating the curative agent in the bark, which is called quinine. It became possible after 1820 to obtain quinine powder to be taken in prescribed dosages. Quinine became widely available in the 1850s, when the Dutch began to cultivate the bark in Java. It is no exaggeration to say that the mass production and distribution of quinine made possible the subsequent European "scramble for Africa."

Empires that Egypt was a key to the security of their Asian possessions. They further understood that the Nile was the key to the livelihood and security of Egypt. By the middle of the nineteenth century, the security of Egypt became even more important when the European powers started building the Suez Canal. This waterway would cut through Egypt to connect the Mediterranean and the Red Seas in 1869.

Missionaries in East Africa had heard about a great inland body of water and snowcapped mountains along the equator. If this lake and these mountains existed, thought European geographers, they could be the source for the Nile River. In 1856, the Royal Geographical Society sponsored an expedition to find the inland lake. Richard Burton led this expedition. Burton was joined by John Hanning Speke. Both men had records of disastrous explorations behind them.

Burton and Speke had served as officers in the Army of India. Speke had joined the Indian army in 1844. He fought in the Punjab in the north of the country. Speke's primary interest in exploration was big-game hunting. Burton, on the other hand, was an accomplished geographer and linguist. Burton and Speke undertook their first journey together in Somalia in 1854. They were ambushed one night in their tents. Burton had a spear thrown through his cheeks. It knocked out four of his teeth. Speke was captured. He eventually escaped, having been wounded 11 times. With their supplies stolen or destroyed, and many of their servants in flight, Burton and Speke abandoned their expedition and returned to England. In 1857 they were off again to East Africa. They were now on the hunt for the source of the Nile.

In June, the two men and a column of over a hundred porters set off from the coastal town of Bagamoyo. This town was one of the most common departure points for European expeditions into central Africa. They immediately encountered difficulties. The men suffered from diseases. After a couple of months, Speke was almost blind. His efforts to kill a beetle that had crawled into his ear while he slept had left him deaf in one ear. Burton had also lost much of his sight. He could no longer walk due to the paralysis of his legs. The two men nonetheless became the first Europeans to encounter Lake Tanganyika. Unfortunately, they could barely see it and were unable to explore its shores. The local African tribes told them that the lake had an outlet to the north. Burton and Speke could not figure out whether this outlet flowed out or in. In fact, this issue would not be settled until 1872. In that year, Henry Morton Stanley and David Livingstone circumnavigated the lake.

Burton and Speke decided to return to the coast to recover their health. On the way eastward, Speke regained his strength and much of his sight. Burton remained ill. They heard reports of a great lake to the north, a lake so large that no one knew its length or breadth. Both Africans and Muslim traders simply referred to this body of water as the N'yanza, "the lake."

Speke received Burton's permission to explore this lake on his own. Speke saw the southern tip of the lake on July 30, 1858. He then gained his first full view of the lake on August 3. Speke recalled that he reached the summit of a hill, "when the vast expanse of the pale-blue waters of the N'yanza burst suddenly upon my gaze." It looked like an inland sea. He was unable to measure the distances of the shores.

This view was one which, even in a well-known and explored country, would have arrested the traveler by its peaceful beauty. The islands, each swelling in a gentle slope to a rounded summit, clothed in wood between the rugged angular closely-cropping rocks of granite, seemed mirrored in the calm surface of the lake; on which I here and there detected a small black speck, the tiny canoe of some Muanza fisherman. . . . The pleasure of the mere view vanished in the presence of those more intense and exciting emotions which are called up by the consideration of the commercial and geographical importance of the prospect before me.

Speke immediately decided that this lake must be the legendary source of the Nile. He stated, "I no longer felt any doubt that the lake at my feet gave birth to that interesting river, the source of which has been the subject of so much speculation, and the object of so many explorers." Speke named the lake Victoria, after the British queen. He then hurried back to tell Burton. Burton refused to believe that the Nile flowed from a lake that he had never seen. He continued to dispute this issue with Speke for several years. Burton believed that the Nile probably originated from Lake Tanganyika. Of course, this lake was one he had taken a hand in discovering.

In 1858, after an arduous journey to locate Africa's Great Lakes—in which he went temporarily blind and deaf—John Hanning Speke (*above*) and Richard Burton were the first known Westerners to find Lake Tanganyika. Later, Speke located Lake Victoria in East Africa, which would prove to be the source of the Nile.

In an effort to settle the matter, the Royal Geographical Society sent Speke back to Lake Victoria in 1860. This time, James Augustus Grant went with him. They proceeded north along the lake and became the first Europeans to enter the African kingdom of Buganda in 1862. Once more traveling alone, Speke proceeded to the northern end of the lake. Local people told him that a river left the lake at what they called "the stones." These stones turned out to be a waterfall. In his *Journal of the Discovery of the Source of the Nile*, Speke described the falls as about 12 feet (3.6 m) high and 400 to 500 feet (121 to 152 m) across, broken by rocks.

> *It was a sight that attracted one to it for hours—the roar of the waters, the thousands of passenger fish, leaping at the falls with all their might; the Wasoga and Waganda fishermen coming out in boats and taking posts on all the rocks with rod and hook, hippopotami and crocodiles lying sleepily on the water, the ferry at work above the falls, and cattle driven down to drink on the margin of the lake—made, in all, with the pretty nature of the country—small hills, grassy topped, with trees in the folds, and gardens on the lower slopes—as interesting a picture as one could wish to see.*

Speke renamed "the stones" the Ripon Falls after the man who had been the head of the Royal Geographical Society when his expedition was first organized. "The expedition had now performed its functions," Speke concluded. "I saw that old father Nile without any doubt rises in the Victoria N'yanza, and, as I had foretold, that lake is the great source of the holy river which cradled the first expounder of our religious belief."

Speke returned to meet Grant and told him of his discovery at the northern end of the lake. Unfortunately, the men no longer had the supplies necessary to follow the river downstream. Moreover, they were unable to investigate reports of another outlet in the northeast corner of the lake leading to another lake beyond. Speke and Grant traveled overland to reconnect with the Nile farther north. Then they traveled by boat to the town of Khartoum. Imagine their surprise when they returned to the Nile and met Speke's old friend, Samuel Baker.

BAKER AND VON SASS FIND THE SECOND SOURCE OF THE NILE

Samuel Baker was traveling with a young woman named Florence von Sass. The two were as unlikely a couple as one might hope to meet in central Africa. Baker was a gentleman of independent wealth who enjoyed traveling and hunting. He had been married. His wife had died, leaving him in his mid-thirties with four children. He had placed these children in the care of his wife's sister. Then he set out from Britain to hunt wild boar and other game in eastern Europe and Asia. During a trip in present-day Bulgaria he saw a group of Hungarians up for sale at a slave auction. Among this group was a 15-year-old, blonde-haired woman. She caught Baker's attention, probably because of her youthful beauty. Baker purchased the woman and they fell in love. Baker did not mention Florence to his family in Britain. He delayed his return home year after year. In the course of these delays, he became intrigued by the idea of finding the source of the Nile, so he organized an expedition.

Samuel and Florence set off up the Nile from Cairo in 1861. They left their boat at Korosko and then rode camels across the Nubian Desert. They explored the rivers leading into the Blue Nile, then proceeded to Khartoum in order to travel up the White Nile. They reached Gondokoro, which Samuel described as "a perfect hell," filled with cutthroats who made their living selling slaves, guns, and liquor. Under the influence of the locals, the men in the Bakers' expedition became unruly. At one point, Samuel confronted the ringleader of the unruly men on the dock beside their boat, resulting in an open brawl. Samuel fought to restore order. Florence emerged from the boat and pushed her way through the fight, yelling at the men to stand back. The men greeted Florence's courage with stunned silence. She negotiated a settlement that enabled Samuel and his adversaries to save face. For the rest of the trip, Florence showed a greater gift for diplomacy than the short-tempered Samuel.

Samuel and Florence prepared to depart upriver. They suddenly heard guns firing in the distance.

Debono's ivory porters arriving, for whom I have waited. My men rushed madly to my boat, with a report that two white men

were with them who had come from the sea! Could they be Speke
and Grant? Off I ran, and soon met them in reality; hurrah for
old England!! They had come from the Victorian Nyanza, from
which the Nile springs . . . The mystery of ages solved.

Samuel was disappointed that his own objective had already been achieved. Speke and Grant then told him about the lake to the west of Victoria. Grant even provided Samuel and Florence with a map. Samuel stated, "Speke expressed his conviction that the Luta N'zige must be a second source of the Nile, and that geographers would be dissatisfied that he had not explored it. To me this was most gratifying."

Samuel and Florence headed toward the rumored lake. They joined a merchant caravan and traveled 180 miles (289 km) overland. In the midst of the journey, when the caravan was crossing a river, Samuel looked back to see Florence drop into the reeds, as if shot dead. She had suddenly contracted a fever. For days she lay unconscious and then delirious. The caravan could not stop due to lack of food, so Florence was carried forward on a litter (stretcher). Samuel sat up each night to watch her for any sign of recovery, but her condition appeared hopeless. As the African porters prepared to dig her grave, Florence regained consciousness and, slowly, her strength. The caravan pressed on. With the assistance of a chief named Kamrasi, Samuel and Florence finally reached the lake in March 1864.

They emerged from the forest about 1,500 feet (457 m) above the lake. Then they descended on a zigzag path for about two hours. Although weakened by fever, Florence insisted on walking this final stretch to the lake with Samuel. She clung to his arm for balance. "A walk of about a mile through flat sandy meadows of fine turf interspersed with trees and bush, brought us to the water's edge," Samuel recalled.

The waves were rolling upon a white pebbly beach: I rushed
into the lake, and thirsty with heat and fatigue, with a heart
full of gratitude, I drank deeply from the Sources of the Nile.
No European foot had ever trod upon its sand, nor had the
eyes of a white man ever scanned its vast expanse of water. We
were the first; and this was the key to the great secret that even
Julius Caesar yearned to unravel, but in vain. Here was the

great basin of the Nile that received every drop of water, even from the passing shower to the roaring mountain torrent that drained from Central Africa towards the north. This was the great reservoir of the Nile!

Samuel named it Lake Albert, in honor of the husband of Queen Victoria. Samuel and Florence were both struck down by fever at Lake Albert. In order to save their lives, they departed for home. They left one geographical question unanswered. It appeared that a river flowing into Lake Albert from the northeast was the Nile. However, they were not sure of this. In addition, there was another river leaving the lake from the west. An American, Charles Chaillé-Long, later solved these questions. In the 1870s, he followed 100 miles (160 km) of the uncharted Nile, proving that the Nile entered and left Lake Albert.

The Nile River is the longest river in the world. The Nile River flows northward from the Sudanese capital Khartoum where two rivers—the Blue and White Niles—meet. Since ancient times, European explorers had searched for the river's source. Today, nearly all of the cultural and historical sites of ancient Egypt are found along the banks of the Nile River.

Samuel and Florence returned to Cairo. Samuel found letters awaiting him at the British consulate. Among the various letters was one from the Royal Geographical Society informing him that he had been awarded the Victoria Gold Medal. The couple was married in London in November 1865. Samuel was knighted in 1866. Given the unseemly background of Baker's wife, Queen Victoria would not permit him to bring her to the ceremony. Florence nevertheless became Lady Baker.

THE EFFECTS OF EXPLORATION OF THE NILE

The European explorations of the Niger and Nile rivers had important consequences for the peoples of Africa. In the near term, European travel to and along these rivers confirmed the ongoing brutalities of the slave trade. This caused European governments to take further action to stop it. The large expeditions of Burton, Speke, Grant, and Stanley also helped to create a new and profitable form of work for Africans. An increasing number of Africans became porters and captains. Their work expanded the interaction between African peoples. It drew Africans to the caravan routes and their major stops.

In the long term, the explorations of the Niger and the Nile opened paths for Europeans into the African interior. Europeans expanded trade and set up missionary stations to spread the Christian faith. Greater access to the African interior produced greater competition and aggression between Europeans and indigenous rulers. It also increased competition between Europeans themselves. In 1898, Britain and France almost went to war for control of the upper Nile.

Europe's expansion down the Niger and up the Nile was not merely a process of economic exploitation, religious conversion, and conquest. As European powers asserted their authority in these regions, they were followed by professional and amateur scientists and, particularly in Egypt, by archaeologists. These researchers located, unearthed, and documented tombs, temples, and cities of the ancient Egyptian kings and queens. They laid the foundations for the field of Egyptology. Unfortunately, these scientists found themselves competing against grave robbers. The robbers would make money plundering and selling ancient artifacts to private collectors in Europe.

One of the most successful champions of ancient Egypt's legacy proved to be a British woman, Amelia Edwards. She was a writer who traveled to Egypt in 1873–1874. Edwards was inspired by the Egyptian monuments that she saw. She was also alarmed by the evidence of their destruction. Upon her return, she published a travel memoir, *A Thousand Miles up the Nile.* She also pushed, prodded, and organized scientists and museum curators to found the Egypt Exploration Society. This group is still at work today funding scientific excavations and the preservation of the monuments of ancient Egypt.

5

Taming the Heart of Darkness

Joseph Conrad's book *Heart of Darkness* opens on the river Thames in England. Several men wait aboard a boat for the tide to carry them out to sea. As the dusk falls, one of the men begins to tell a tale about his earlier travels in central Africa. He recalls that as a boy he looked at maps of the world and dreamed of traveling to the blank spaces. Africa had been the biggest of those blank spaces, but that had changed by the end of the nineteenth century. "It had filled since my boyhood with rivers and lakes and names," Marlow observes. "It had ceased to be a blank space of delightful mystery—a white patch for a boy to dream gloriously over. It had become a place of darkness."

In the 1800s every schoolchild had heard of the forbidden place known then as the "Dark Continent." Most people identified Africa with its heart: a vast region of great lakes, rivers, and dense jungle. Central Africa was a place of myth and mystery in the minds of Europeans. They imagined a place overrun by wild beasts, cannibals, and slave traders. To them it represented all that was uncivilized, all that was savage. It also represented hope. It represented future profits, conversions to the Christian faith, and adventure.

Children dreamt of Africa. Some grew up to become explorers who cut through Africa's jungles and rode down its rivers in canoes. As they advanced, however, myths gave way to realities. Europeans took far more from central Africa than they gave in return. They exploited resources and labor in exchange, too often, for only liquor and guns or for relief from conquest. By the end of the century, central

Africa had, indeed, become a place of darkness, but a darkness of the Europeans' making.

CROSSING AFRICA

Commerce and Christianity were the driving forces behind exploration in central Africa. In the 1840s, Dr. David Livingstone had decided that he must try to find a natural highway from the coastline into the interior. On such a highway, missionary stations, trading factories, and perhaps, someday, colonial settlements might prosper.

Livingstone set out northward from Kolobeng, South Africa, in April 1850. His wife and three children traveled with him. He was also joined by a fellow missionary, William Oswell and a local chief, Sechele. They proceeded into the land of the Makololo. There they established excellent relations with the chief, Sebituane, who welcomed their proposal to establish a mission station in his kingdom. The chief died before he could assist Livingstone. He was succeeded by his daughter, Mamochisane, who intended to honor her father's wishes. With this new chief's blessing, Livingstone's small expedition proceeded into central Africa, arriving at Sesheke in June 1851. There they came upon a surprising sight: the Zambezi River, one of the great rivers of Africa. This river might be the "highway" Livingstone was looking for.

"This was an important point," Livingstone observed, "for that river was not previously known to exist there at all." It was the dry season, but the width of the river was 300 to 600 yards (274 to 584 m) of deep water. The region around Sesheke was marshy and fever-ridden. The local people lived there because the inhospitable land provided protection from slave traders. Livingstone suspected that farther upriver he might find a more suitable area for his missionary station. Livingstone recalls, "I at once resolved to save my family from exposure to this unhealthy region by sending them to England, and to return alone, with a view to exploring the country in search of a healthy district that might prove a centre of civilization, and open up the interior by a path to either the east or west coast."

Livingstone returned to Cape Town and sent his family home. He wasted no time in setting off northward from the cape in June 1852. He returned to the land of the Makololo, where he again enjoyed a generous reception. He met with Mamochisane and a new chief, an

18-year-old man named Sekelutu. With Sekelutu's support, Living-stone returned to Sesheke. He journeyed up the Zambezi with 33 canoes. He proceeded easily through Makololo territory. His good fortune continued until early in 1854. That is when he left the upper reaches of the Zambezi and crossed the watershed between the Zam-bezi and the Congo rivers.

He had not yet found an area suitable for a mission station, but he was still hopeful that he might find one if he proceeded west. He encountered two black Portuguese slave traders, Silva Porto and Caetano Ferra. They told him about a route followed by slave caravans to Luanda, Angola, in West Africa. Livingstone followed this route, but he soon suffered from the fear and hostility that slave traders had cre-ated along the way.

The expedition finally made it to a Portuguese outpost. The offi-cers fed and clothed Livingstone and his men. They also provided them with a guide to the coast. The final march was arduous. Livingstone was nearly killed by hunger and fever as he staggered to the coast. He probably would have died had it not been for a ship's surgeon who cared for him for several weeks. The Europeans at Luanda and along the West African coast hailed Livingstone's heroism. The news of his expedition made headlines in British newspapers. However, Livingstone felt that his work was not finished. He had not yet found a site for a mission, nor a safe route into the African interior. To the amazement of his Euro-pean hosts at Luanda, he bought more supplies and returned east.

Livingstone reached the upper Zambezi in 1855. His expedition traveled down the Zambezi in canoes until they heard rumors about a nearby land. It was said to be rich in plants and wildlife. It was also supposed to be free from malaria, the tsetse fly, and even the slave trade. Livingstone left the river to investigate with men from the Batoka tribe to guide him. They led Livingstone to a plateau about 1,000 miles (1,609 km) from the coast. Livingstone was excited to discover an excel-lent site for a mission. The Batoka told him, "No one ever dies of hunger here." Livingstone described what he saw:

> *The plain below us . . . had more large game on it than any where else I had seen in Africa. Hundreds of buffaloes and zebras grazed on the open spaces, and there stood lordly elephants*

David Livingstone became one of the most famous explorers of the nineteenth century. He died in Africa, and his servants remained loyal. They buried his heart and internal organs at the foot of a tree, and then carried his preserved body all the way to the coast for transport back to Britain. He is still honored throughout the world in various ways, including this statue that stands on the Zambezi River at Victoria Falls.

feeding majestically. . . . I wished that I had been able to take a photograph of a scene so seldom beheld, and which is destined, as guns increase, to pass away from the earth.

Livingstone was anxious to carry news of his discovery to the coast. Unfortunately, he returned to the Zambezi at a point far to the east of where he had left the river. He wrongly assumed that the river was navigable between these points. In fact, that part of the river contained a dangerous series of rapids. Livingstone might easily have taken measurements of altitude on the river. These would have shown that there was a drop caused by either rapids or waterfalls. In one fateful moment of distraction, Livingstone forgot to perform the calculations essential to exploration.

He arrived at the mouth of the Zambezi in May 1856. Even though the Zambezi was not the natural highway Livingstone thought he had found, the expedition was still important. Livingston had covered 5,000 miles (8,046 km). He had completed the first crossing of sub-Saharan Africa by a European.

Livingstone returned to the Zambezi in 1858. His wife, artists, scientists, and two photographers joined him. The group traveled up the Zambezi toward the Batoka Plateau, but it was stopped by the rapids Livingstone had overlooked two years earlier. The expedition then experienced a series of calamities that were only made worse by Livingstone's refusal to quit. Livingstone's wife died of fever, and diseases overtook other members of the party.

Livingstone now knew that the Zambezi was not a highway into central Africa. Boats could not reach the lands near the Batoka Plateau. So, he began looking for another location for European settlement. He believed that he had found such a place on land that came to be called the Shire Highlands. The British government, however, refused to pay for the settlement. Livingstone then invited the Universities Mission to establish a station in the Highlands. The mission sent its brethren, many of whom quickly died of disease.

By 1863, the British government had lost all confidence in Livingstone's judgment and cut off his funds. In January, a newspaper called Livingstone's Zambezi expedition a waste of money: "We were promised cotton, sugar and indigo, and of course we got none. We were promised converts and not one has been made. In a word, the thousands subscribed have been productive only of the most fatal results."

A lesser explorer would have been ruined by this experience. Livingstone, however, returned to Britain. He gathered support for another expedition, this time in search of the source of the Nile River. (See Chapter 4.) He arrived in Africa in 1865 and died there in 1873, at the height of his fame.

A SEAMAN TRAVELS OVERLAND

It seemed unlikely that a man who had made his living on the sea would be the first European to walk across Africa near the equator. Yet this was just what Verney Lovett Cameron did. Cameron joined the British

PHOTOGRAPHY IN AFRICA

Soon after the invention of photography in 1839, explorers wanted to put this new technology to use. Sir John Herschel, an English astronomer, tried to take photographs during a British expedition in the Antarctic. He failed due to the cumbersome equipment, the fragile glass plates upon which the images were made, and the cold. Fortunately, explorers took up new photographic technologies, such as the "wet plate" collodion process, invented by Frederick Scott Archer in 1851.

Photography was not well suited to exploration in Africa. Exposure time for these early cameras could be as long as several minutes, during which subjects had to remain perfectly still in order to avoid blurring the image. David Livingstone nevertheless brought the photographic team of Charles Livingstone and John Kirk on his Zambezi expedition. They experienced numerous difficulties and disappointments in their work. Kirk succeeded in taking a number of landscape photographs. However, Livingstone produced only one picture during the entire journey.

In the 1870s, at the beginning of the so-called scramble for Africa, dry-plate photography was invented. It replaced the

Royal Navy in 1857. He served around the world, from the coast of India to the coast of Louisiana in the United States. Then, in the late 1860s, he was posted to a quiet port in England. He quickly became bored. He dreamed of Africa after reading accounts of the expeditions of Burton, Speke, and Livingstone.

In 1870, while still stationed in England, Cameron tried to persuade the Royal Geographical Society (RGS) to send him on an expedition to find Livingstone. At the time, Livingstone was presumed lost or dead. However, news that Henry Stanley had located Livingstone soon reached Britain. Two years later, the RGS sent Cameron to Africa to help Livingstone and then undertake an independent exploration with Livingstone's assistance. He and several colleagues landed at Zanzibar

wet-plate process. The most important benefit of this new technology was that people could take photographs and develop them later, under controlled conditions. This is not to say that photography in Africa became easy. Arthur Conan Doyle, the creator of Sherlock Holmes, was also an amateur photographer. He traveled to West Africa on a photographic expedition in the late nineteenth century. He experienced great frustration due to the heat and the humidity that weakened the seals of the bottles in which he stored his photographic chemicals.

Photography in Africa was made simpler in 1888. An American, George Eastman, introduced the box camera. He called it the Kodak. This camera captured images on a roll of paper which the photographer mailed to a Kodak lab for developing. The Kodak also featured a faster shutter speed that eliminated the need for a tripod. Finally, just as the creation of photographs was becoming more simple and reliable, their distribution accelerated in the 1890s, when a new method for printing photos in half tones made mass production in the press possible. This method enabled the public to see Africa through photographs in newspapers and magazines.

on the east coast in February 1873. At the coastal town of Bagamoyo they were joined by additional Europeans, including Robert Moffat, a sugar planter who was Livingstone's nephew. They set off toward the Great Lakes region, where Livingstone was last reported.

They were slowed by disease and desertion of their porters. Moffat died of fever. Cameron and the remaining Europeans struggled with fever as well. They were camped and recovering their health when, on October 20, they received a letter from one of Livingstone's servants indicating that Livingstone had died.

Part of Cameron's company chose to accompany the body to the coast but Cameron and a naval surgeon, W. E. Dillon, pushed forward to Ujiji, on Lake Tanganyika. A few weeks later, in a feverish delirium, Dillon shot himself and died. Cameron was having difficulty seeing. He had also recently suffered a back injury when he fell from a donkey. Despite this, he chose again to keep going.

Cameron explored and mapped much of the region around Ujiji. He recorded 96 rivers flowing into Lake Tanganyika and one flowing out of it. The latter river flowed into the Lukuga River. Cameron was told that it then flowed into the Lualaba. Most important, Cameron learned that the Lualaba River probably flowed into the Congo. The Congo is a large river that empties on Africa's west coast. Cameron proceeded westward to follow the Lualaba. He was eager to discover whether it did, in fact, become the Congo.

He followed the Lualaba downstream to Nyangwe. This was the same village where Livingstone had turned back from his quest for the source of the Nile in 1870. Cameron found that the merchants at Nyangwe would not provide him with canoes. It appeared that his expedition was at an end. He then received advice from the most powerful slave trader in this part of Africa, Tippu Tip. Tip advised the explorer to abandon the Lualaba River and proceed south, then west to Angola.

Cameron followed Tip's advice. His expedition soon experienced conflicts with local tribes. In one incident, villagers stole Cameron's goat, named Dinah. Cameron insisted that the goat be returned. In response, the villagers attacked the expedition with arrows and spears. Cameron and his men returned fire with their guns and fled to the next village, where they were again greeted with a rain of arrows and spears. In desperation, Cameron and several of his men charged the village, firing their guns. They drove the inhabitants into the forest. Cameron then fortified the village, naming it Fort Dinah, in honor of his stolen goat. He and his men fought off their attackers for three days. Eventually, a settlement was reached. Cameron's expedition was allowed to carry on.

Cameron and his men entered the realm of King Kasongo. He was a brutal ruler who was away from home in order to terrorize and steal from his subjects. Cameron had to wait for the king's approval to move through the kingdom. In January 1875, Cameron finally met Kasongo. The young king was accompanied by a large number of men. The men were missing ears, hands, and various other body parts. They fawned over the king, singing his praises. Later, Cameron learned that these men had been injured by Kasongo himself. Cameron explains: "Kasongo acts like a demon, ordering death and mutilation indiscriminately and behaving in the most barbarous manner to any who may be near him."

Kasongo told Cameron that he would someday visit England. Until then, Cameron's ruler was to pay him tribute. Kasongo wanted rifles, cannons, and boats. Cameron did his best to intimidate Kasongo with accounts of Queen Victoria's military power and otherwise humor the king and win his confidence. Over the course of many weeks, Cameron asked Kasongo to provide him with guides to take him north to the Congo River. Kasongo ignored these requests. Instead, he insisted that Cameron attend a ceremony in which local chiefs would pay him tribute. Cameron was lucky. He learned that Kasongo planned to attack him during the ceremony and steal his belongings.

Cameron posted 60 men around his camp. He took 60 more with him to meet Kasongo. The ceremony took place. Kasongo sat pompously and received his local chiefs. Cameron's men were on one side, facing their enemies. Kasongo decided to spare his guest, or himself, an ugly battle. He instead delayed Cameron's departure for several more months.

Cameron finally left in June 1875. He joined the slave caravan of José Antonio Alves. Alves had agreed to guide Cameron's expedition to Angola on the coast. "The conduct of Alvez's men on the road was disgraceful," commented Cameron. "They attacked any small parties of natives whom they chanced to meet and plundered their loads, though these consisted chiefly of dried fish and corn which were being carried as tribute to Kasongo." The caravan was under constant threat of attack.

The caravan had left Kasongo's land with more than 1,500 slaves. In July 1875, Cameron was horrified to see one of Alves's men emerge from the forest with 52 women tied together. Many of the women were carrying children. Cameron had been inspired to explore Africa in order to combat slavery. He now found that his life depended on slave traders.

The going became more difficult. The slave traders demanded larger payments from Cameron for guidance and food. When the caravan reached Angola, the slave traders stopped at their base and left Cameron and his men to continue on their own to the coast. Cameron had to sell his own shirts to feed his men. Further on, they were reduced to eating locusts. Suffering from scurvy, Cameron struggled into the

Verney Lovett Cameron was hired to locate David Livingstone and provide support to him in Africa. While traveling, he and his group were informed of Livingstone's death. He made his own explorations and became the first European to cross equatorial Africa from east to west. Here, Cameron is received by Chief Katende in his village during the expedition.

Portuguese station at Katombela on November 7, 1875. A Portuguese official greeted him in disbelief, then opened a bottle of wine to celebrate the first European to walk across Africa from east to west. Cameron was in no condition to celebrate. He was carried to Benguela, on the coast, where a European surgeon saved his life.

Cameron returned to Liverpool in April 1876 and was hailed as the greatest explorer since Livingstone. He was promoted to the rank of commander in the Royal Navy and received gold medals from the Royal Geographical Society and the Geographical Society of Paris. In a lecture tour of Britain, he spoke of the commercial potential of Africa. He reported that Africa might hold great mineral wealth—not only in copper but also in gold, silver, and coal. Cameron believed that the successful development of Africa depended on the progress of both commerce and Christianity.

Cameron would later lead expeditions into the Middle East, seeking a secure overland trade route to Asia. Then, with Richard Burton, he explored West Africa in search of gold mines. In the 1880s he retired from the navy and turned his energies to commercial interests in Africa. In March 1894 he was thrown from a horse and killed.

THE LUALABA BECOMES THE CONGO

Cameron's belief that the Lualaba flowed into the Congo River was soon tested by Henry Stanley. Stanley had become famous by finding Livingstone in 1871. However, geographers did not respect him as an explorer. They thought he just wanted to be famous. Stanley had been awed and inspired by Livingstone, who was regarded as the greatest explorer of his era. When he learned in 1873 that Livingstone had died, he decided to carry on Livingstone's work. He hoped to answer one of the biggest geographical questions of the day: Was the Lualaba the source of the Nile or the Congo? And, if it was the source of the Congo, was it possible to navigate down the river to the west coast? If it was, then the Congo was a highway into the center of the continent.

Stanley obtained funding for his expedition from the New York *Herald Tribune* and London's *Daily Telegraph*. These newspapers had exclusive rights to his reports of his travels. Stanley returned to Africa in 1874 and gathered together his caravan at Bagamoyo. In November, he marched inland at the head of a column of 359 people.

Their progress was difficult from the start. Within just two months, in January 1875, 20 had died, 89 had deserted, and many were sick. Yet Stanley reached Lake Victoria. He assembled a portable boat, the *Lady Alice*, that he had brought from England. In this boat he became the first European to circumnavigate both Lake Victoria and Lake Tanganyika.

Stanley confirmed Cameron's finding that Lake Tanganyika did not empty into the Nile but into the Lukuga River. Stanley traveled to Nyangwe, where Livingstone and Cameron had failed to secure passage down the river. Again, Tippu Tip was at Nyangwe. He and Stanley became friends. Tip guided Stanley down the river with 1,000 men. The jungle along the river was dense, with Stanley sometimes crawling on his hands and knees. To make matters worse, the group was often attacked by local peoples, who had the advantage of knowing the terrain. After about 200 miles (321 km), Tip refused to go any farther and turned back. Stanley and his people continued down the river using the *Lady Alice* and 22 canoes they had acquired both by purchase and combat since leaving Nyangwe.

Stanley's exploration of the river proved to be an epic, often horrifying experience. He and his followers fought almost three dozen battles. Stanley gained a reputation for brutality. However, he avoided far more fights than he engaged. Stanley understood that this was not a military expedition. In fact, Stanley's greatest enemies were the river, disease, and hunger. The group struggled constantly against malaria, typhoid, and dysentery. The river confronted them with impassable waterfalls and rapids. Separating the upper and lower river is a series of 32 rapids, covering about 220 miles (354 km). Stanley had to leave the *Lady Alice* along these rapids and walk the remainder of the way to the sea.

Stanley successfully proved that the Lualaba flowed into the Congo River. He entered the European outpost at Boma in August 1877, only 110 miles (177 km) from the coast. Only 82 of the expedition's original 359 people returned. Stanley wrote about his exploration in *Through the Dark Continent*, which became a best seller. No one would again question Stanley's status as one of the greatest explorers of the nineteenth century.

Upon Stanley's return to Europe, he was approached by King Leopold II of Belgium, who had become interested in the commercial prospects of central Africa after Cameron's transcontinental journey.

Stanley agreed to work on behalf of the king and went back to the Congo in 1878. Stanley worked for the next five years to secure the south bank of the Congo River, building stations and trading networks, both by order and by example. He received the nickname Bula Matari ("breaker of rocks") from African laborers who watched him swing a hammer in road construction. Stanley left King Leopold's service in 1884, having laid the foundation of the Congo Free State, which Leopold established in the following year.

THE EFFECTS OF EXPLORATION OF CENTRAL AFRICA

The European exploration of central Africa had almost immediate consequences for the peoples of the region. Within just a year of his successful exploration of the Congo, Stanley laid the foundation for a European imperial regime, the Congo Free State. While Stanley and the other major explorers had justified their work as a campaign against the African slave trade, the empires that they helped to create then exploited Africans through what critics would call "new systems of slavery." Local African rulers, such as those who signed treaties with Stanley, would profit from this exploitation, thus dividing Africans against themselves.

In the middle of the nineteenth century, the European map of Africa had been largely blank except for the coastal regions and the Muslim countries to the North. By the early twentieth century, it was filled by the paths of rivers, which European merchants, missionaries, and generals had followed to lay the boundaries of their empires in the wake of the great explorers.

6

Pilgrimages to Mecca and the Arabian Sands

HARRY ST. JOHN BRIDGER PHILBY WAS MARCHING TOWARD disappointment. He had been waiting for years to explore the Rub' al-Khali, the Empty Quarter, of the Arabian Peninsula in 1932. The Empty Quarter was a large desert in the southern half of the peninsula, one of the few places on Earth still unknown to geographers. He had finally secured the approval and support of the head of the Saudi royal family, Ibn Saud. Now, just five days and 140 miles (225 km) into their journey, Philby's men had lost their nerve.

Had Philby wished only to speed their camel caravan across the desert in the cool of the night, the men would not have been troubled. But Philby saw no point in merely passing through the Empty Quarter. This had been recently done for the first time by another explorer, Bertram Thomas. Since Philby could not be the first European through the Empty Quarter, he now proposed to be the most thorough. He proposed to travel by day along a circuitous route to conduct a meticulous survey of the landscape under the blazing sun. His guides and servants saw no reason in this. There was no prospect of trading or settlement in this desolate region. There was no prospect of mass religious conversion, given that there were few residents of the Empty Quarter. Moreover, Philby himself had already converted to Islam. Actually, Philby's reason was simple: He wanted to be famous. He attempted to rally his men but to no avail. He accompanied the expedition back to their point of departure and then, famously, returned to survey the Empty Quarter with great success throughout the remainder of his life.

THE GEOGRAPHY OF
THE ARABIAN PENINSULA

The Arabian Peninsula is found in the southwestern corner of Asia. It covers an area of about one million square miles (1,609,344 sq km). To the west, the Red Sea separates the peninsula from northeast Africa. The peninsula is then surrounded by the Arabian Sea to the south and the Sea of Oman and the Persian Gulf to the northeast. The southern and eastern coastlines are occupied by Muslim states, including Yemen. In the eighteenth and nineteenth centuries, the northern boundary of the peninsula was marked by Palestine (now Israel and the Palestinian Territories), Syria, Persia (now Iraq), and Kuwait.

Most of the peninsula was divided between two areas. The Hejaz was the fertile region on the west coast. It held the Muslim holy sites of Mecca and Medina. The Hejaz had long been active in the trade networks between Africa and Asia. East of the Hejaz was the Nejd. This was a large, dry region. It was bordered by the Nafúd Desert to the north and the Empty Quarter to the south. In the early nineteenth century, the Nejd remained virtually unknown to Europeans.

European overseas exploration had begun during an era of intense rivalry between Christianity and Islam. As the modern era of exploration began in the eighteenth century, the balance of power in this rivalry was shifting in favor of Europe's Christian powers. By the mid-nineteenth century, the British usurped the power of the emperor in South Asia, and the Russians conquered most of the khanates and emirates in Central Asia. In eastern Europe and the Middle East, the Ottoman Empire, with its center of power in present-day Turkey, was threatened by the growing industries and modern militaries of both western Europe and Russia. Most of the Arabian Peninsula was subject to the Ottoman ruler, who held the dual position of sultan and caliph. The first title defined his political authority, and the second designated his spiritual authority as the leader of Muslims around the world. It was crucially important that the Ottoman ruler maintain his control over the Muslim holy sites, especially Mecca and Medina, located in western Arabia.

From the eighteenth century until the 1930s, European exploration of the Arabian Peninsula took place in the midst of violent political turmoil. In the eighteenth century, a group seeking religious reform grew strong. Known as the Wahhabi movement, they gained strength in central Arabia and allied with the Saudi dynasty. They then declared a new state in defiance of the Ottoman Empire. In 1802, Prince Saud I captured Mecca, and in 1804 he captured Medina, asserting Wahhabi authority over most of the peninsula. The Ottoman sultan responded by appointing a new ruler in Egypt, Muhammad 'Ali Pasha, whose forces reoccupied Mecca and Medina in 1812. The Ottomans put down the Wahhabi uprising in 1815. However, it rose again in the Nejd, declaring an independent state in 1824. The Wahhabi movement again collapsed in 1891, only to be restored to power by Ibn Saud, the future patron of Philby, in 1902.

LEARNING ABOUT THE PEOPLE OF ARABIA

At first, Europeans' interest in the Arabian Peninsula lay only in its coasts. Most of the Arabian Peninsula remained unvalued and, therefore, unexplored by Europeans. There were certainly those who took a scientific interest in the interior regions of Arabia, but they were generally discouraged by reports of unforgiving desert terrain, terrible heat, and the Bedouin (nomadic peoples of the Nejd who Europeans considered savage). Many Europeans had heard of Mecca and Medina. However, the few Europeans who had visited these places were almost all converts to Islam and indifferent to exploration.

In the 1750s, Frederik V, the king of Denmark, sponsored an expedition to Yemen. At the time, this was the most familiar part of Arabia. Carsten Niebuhr, a German engineer and surveyor, led the expedition. He was accompanied by an artist, a botanist, a zoologist, an Orientalist scholar, and a former soldier, who acted as a servant. In 1760, the expedition sailed from Copenhagen, Denmark, to Egypt. It stayed there for one year as its members improved their Arabic and made additional preparations for their journey. They then sailed on a boat loaded with pilgrims to the port city of Loheia in Yemen. After four months on the coast, they traveled inland on donkeys. The men stopped often at village coffee shops for refreshment. Although they did not attempt to conceal their identities as Europeans, they did try to adapt to the culture of the Yemeni people. Niebuhr traveled in Yemeni clothes, with a saber and two pistols in his belt. A bucket of water hung from the piece of carpet that was his saddle. They reached the town of Beit el-Fakih, a central coffee market, and decided to make this their base. From here they visited foothills and fertile valleys, admiring the many coffee plantations that were the basis of the local economy.

They proceeded eastward into the mountains, which rose to heights of 8,000 feet (2,438 m). They often found themselves traveling upon well-maintained roads, some of which were paved. They enjoyed the hospitality of the many villages in the area. Unfortunately, despite the beauty and security of their journeys, a couple of members of the expedition died of disease during these travels.

After several months the expedition moved northward to Sana, Yemen's capital. This time they assumed Arab names and the appearance of Arab Christians. The city was small enough to walk around in just one day. It featured several impressive mosques and many palaces built of burnt bricks and cut stones. Beyond the city walls was a beautiful garden and, beyond, a fertile region where one found many kinds of fruit, including 12 varieties of grapes. Niebuhr and his colleagues were welcomed by the ruler of Yemen, al-Mahdi 'Abbas bin al-Mansur Husain. He gave them money, new clothes, and camels. Not wanting to overstay their welcome, the Europeans left Sana after less than a week aboard an English merchant ship bound for Bombay. As they sailed across the Indian Ocean, the last of Niebuhr's European companions died. Niebuhr nonetheless reached India. He sent home his journals, then traveled back to Europe through Persia, Armenia, and Asia Minor, arriving in Denmark in 1767.

Niebuhr published his book, *Description of Arabia*, in German in 1772. He described the Arabs as a noble and hospitable people with a complex culture. Most important, he rejected the common European belief of the time that Muslims were naturally bent upon the destruction of Christianity. On the contrary, he assured Europe's Christians that Muslims generally did not persecute people of other religions unless those people gave them something to fear.

TO MECCA

While European merchants focused primarily on the southern Arabian Peninsula, European imperial governments were interested in Mecca. Every year, millions of Muslims undertook the hajj. This is the

Since the seventh century, Mecca, the holiest city of the Islamic faith, has hosted millions of pilgrims who are participating in the hajj (holy pilgrimage). One of the rituals performed during the hajj includes walking counter-clockwise around the Kaaba, the black cube-shaped building in the center that acts as the Muslim direction of prayer.

pilgrimage to Mecca that each Muslim is to complete at least once in his or her lifetime. Europeans also went on the hajj. Some went as Muslim converts. Others were sent by their nations' rulers. In 1814, Johann Ludwig Burckhardt reached Mecca on behalf of the British. He was actually trying to reach the Niger River in Africa.

Burckhardt was born in Switzerland and educated in Germany. After completing his education, he went to Britain with a letter of introduction to Sir Joseph Banks, the explorer and founder of the Association for Promoting the Discovery of the Interior Parts of Africa. Banks was impressed by Burckhardt and arranged for the association to sponsor him on an exploratory mission. The goal of this mission was the discovery of the source of the Niger River. Burckhardt was asked to reach the river through the Middle East and North Africa.

In comparison with the elaborate preparations for other expeditions, Burckhardt's preparations appear naïve. For six weeks prior to his departure, Burckhardt attended an assortment of academic lectures on topics ranging from botany to astronomy, he studied Arabic, and he took long walks without a hat. He departed in 1809 for Syria, pausing for two months at Malta in order to improve his Arabic and to assemble a disguise as an Indian Muslim trader. He then sailed on to Aleppo, where he stayed for longer than two years to become fluent in Arabic. He also traveled through Syria and Palestine and even located the ruins of the ancient city of Petra in present-day Jordan.

After further travels in Palestine and Egypt, Burckhardt sailed to Arabia in 1814. He was disguised as an Egyptian, using the name Ibrahim ibn Abdallah. Burckhardt experienced serious financial difficulties, but fortunately he was befriended by Muhammad 'Ali, pasha of Egypt. Ali was in Arabia battling the Wahhabi. Burckhardt told Ali that he wanted to visit Mecca as a Muslim pilgrim. The pasha agreed to allow Burckhardt to make the trip on the condition that Burckhardt demonstrate that he understood Islam. Burckhardt passed an exam by two scholars of Islamic law and recited a long chapter from the Koran. He was therefore permitted to perform the rites of the hajj, which he did with respect and reverence for his extraordinary opportunity.

Burckhardt stayed in Mecca for four months. He then visited Medina, the other major holy site of the Hejaz. This is where the prophet Muhammad formed his first community and was later buried. Having spent several years in the Middle East, Burckhardt finally turned to his preparations for an expedition to locate the source of the Niger River. Before he could begin the journey, he contracted dysentery and died in Cairo in 1817. He was buried in a Muslim cemetery. His grave was marked by the name he used in his travels, Ibrahim ibn Abdallah.

WALKING ACROSS THE PENINSULA

The first European to cross the Arabian Peninsula did so by accident. Captain George Sadlier was sent from India in 1819 on a diplomatic mission. Sadlier was to congratulate the pasha on his suppression of a rebellion in Arabia and to propose joint action against the pirates of Muscat, who were then a threat to European shipping in the Sea of Oman. He sailed into the Persian Gulf and landed on the east coast of the peninsula. Unfortunately, he missed the pasha. The Egyptian forces had already moved west. Sadlier spent three months chasing the pasha and his army and caught up with them at Medina. From there he traveled to Yanbu on the west coast and then sailed back to India via the Red Sea. By all accounts, Sadlier would have gladly foregone the honor of crossing the Arabian Peninsula. He detested the place and its peoples.

A far more enthusiastic explorer, William Gifford Palgrave, became the first European to travel eastward across the peninsula in 1862. Ordained as a Jesuit priest, in 1853 Palgrave began missionary work in Syria. He was forced to flee Syria after a massacre of Christians at Damascus in 1861. However, he returned just a year later to begin a journey through central Arabia. For this journey he disguised himself as a Syrian doctor, going by the name Mahmoud el-Eys.

Palgrave was working for Pope Pius IX. The pope hoped to spread Christianity in the Middle East. Palgrave also worked for the French ruler, Napoleon III, who wanted to form alliances with Arab leaders and trade for Arabian horses. Both leaders were anticipating the completion of the Suez Canal in 1869. This waterway would improve European access to the Arabian Peninsula and to the region at large.

Palgrave and another Catholic priest left from the west coast city of Ma'an on camels. They were joined by a guide and several servants. In his memoir, *A Year's Journey through Central and Eastern Arabia,* Palgrave wrote about the discomfort and frustration of traveling in a camel caravan: "[The camel] will never attempt to throw you off his back, such a trick being far beyond his limited comprehension; but if you fall off, he will never dream of stopping for you, and walks on just the same, grazing while he goes, without knowing or caring an atom what has become of you."

At this time, central Arabia was divided between warring factions. The Saudi dynasty attempted to maintain its dominance over the region. Palgrave reached Riyadh, the capital of the house of Saud where he stayed for almost six weeks. Although the Saudis were willing to deal with him, the Wahhabi religious leaders were deeply suspicious of Palgrave's intentions. As usual during his travels, he provided

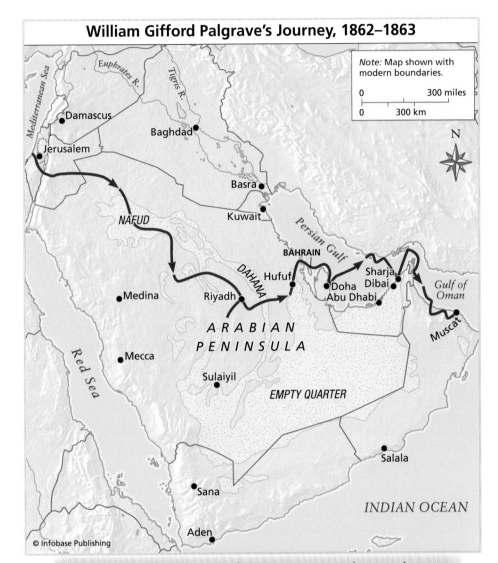

William Gifford Palgrave's Journey, 1862–1863

Note: Map shown with modern boundaries.

William Gifford Palgrave was the first European to travel eastward across the Arabian Peninsula in 1862. He had the support of Pope Pius IX, who wanted to spread Christianity in the Middle East, and Napoleon III, who wanted more information about Arabia in order for France to gain access to Africa and the Middle East.

medical care to those in need. His medical skills soon came to the attention of a member of the Saudi royal family, Prince 'Abd-Allah. The prince asked Palgrave to provide him with poison, which he probably intended to administer to his brother, his archrival. When

Palgrave refused, the prince then called him to his palace. Palgrave recounted the interview:

> *After an interval of silence, 'Abd-Allah turned half round towards me, and with his blackest look and a deep voice said, "I now know perfectly well what you are; you are no doctors, you are Christians, spies, and revolutionists come hither to ruin our religion and state on behalf of those who sent you. The penalty for such as you is death, that you know, and I am determined to inflict it without delay.*

Palgrave denied the prince's charges and managed to bluff his way out of the palace. He and his companions remained in Riyadh for two more days, and then fled the city. They made it to the east coast and immediately boarded a ship to safety. After a few years, Palgrave left the Jesuit order to become a British diplomat in northeast Africa and the Middle East. He died of bronchitis as the minister-resident in Uruguay in 1888, having returned once more to the Catholic faith.

IN SEARCH OF HORSES

Unlike William Palgrave, Sir Wilfrid and Lady Anne Blunt traveled easily through the deserts of the Arabian Peninsula. Lady Anne was the granddaughter of Lord Byron, one of the great British poets of the nineteenth century. She married Blunt, a fellow aristocrat, in 1869 and enjoyed a comfortable existence. In the mid-1870s, the Blunts traveled in Egypt, the Sinai, and Jerusalem. In 1878, they assembled a large camel caravan at Aleppo and marched inland in search of horses. They followed the Euphrates River eastward to Baghdad, then traveled north. They followed the Tigris River until Shergha. There they turned west. At the Khabur River they then turned southwest to Damascus, then back to the Mediterranean coast. Lady Anne became the first European woman to visit the Nejd on the Arabian Peninsula.

There were several bloody wars among the Bedouins in the regions of the Blunts' travels. The couple was most concerned about the threat of a Bedouin raiding party, known as a ghazú. Lady Anne felt certain that they could fight off a ghazú of up to 15 men. After all, she reasoned, the Bedouin had only lances and old pistols. Wilfrid carried a

Winchester rifle that could fire 14 cartridges without being reloaded. If they met a larger threat, the Blunts would simply abandon their possessions. As Lady Blunt coolly reflected in her travel memoir, *Bedouin Tribes of the Euphrates* (1879):

> *At the worst, according to every account, there is no fear of being personally ill-treated; for the Arabs only care about plunder, and the utmost misfortune that could happen to us, if captured, would be to be stripped of some of our clothes, and left to find our way on foot to the nearest inhabited place—not a cheerful prospect, certainly, by still not altogether desperate.*

Lady Anne knew that they faced a greater threat from the desert, which on more than one occasion appeared to be, as she put it, "a simmering furnace." The greatest dangers were to become lost or to run out of water

THE BEDOUIN

The Bedouin are people of the various migratory tribes on the Arabian Peninsula. The word *Bedouin* comes from an Arabic word, *Bedu*, which means "inhabitants of the desert." The Bedouins are not a single ethnic clan, or tribal group. They do share a migratory way of life and a mixed economy. They farm during certain months. During the remainder of the year they herd camels, cattle, sheep, and goats.

In pre-Islamic Arabia, the Bedouin held a lot of power. Most significant was a Bedouin tribal kingdom, Kindah, which was located in the southern part of the Arabian Peninsula in present-day Yemen. Since the end of World War I, when many of the contemporary states, or at least the political boundaries, of the Middle East were established, the Bedouin have been in conflict with modern political organizations. Bedouins are scattered among several states in the contemporary Middle East, including Egypt, Israel, Saudi Arabia, Iraq, Syria, and Jordan. They are a small minority group in each country, often with little power. They nonetheless sustain their tribal organizations.

between the wells that marked the caravan routes. In the book she later wrote called *Bedouin Tribes*, Lady Anne described a day when she and Wilfrid realized that their caravan was about to become separated:

> *It was just about noon, and the mirage in the middle of the day quickly swallows up even a caravan of camels on the horizon, or they get hidden in a dip of the plain, and ours were now out of sight. Wilfrid and I galloped on to keep up the line of communication, which it is very dangerous to lose in traveling in the desert; and it was well we did so, for by the time we sighted them the rest of our straggling party was, in its turn, lost to view.*

Lady Anne rode ahead to stop the caravan. Wilfrid rode back to collect the stragglers. It was lucky he did. They had veered off in the wrong direction.

The Blunts did not rely upon tools of navigation in the desert. Instead, they used Bedouin methods. They would march toward a "tell," something on the horizon that could keep them on a relatively straight course. They also learned to make use of the sun and the wind. "The shadow of one's horse's neck makes an excellent dial," Lady Anne explained, "and with a little practice it is easy to calculate the rate at which it ought to move round so that the course should be a straight one. The wind, too, in this country almost always blows north-west, and does not shift about in the plain, as it would among hills."

The Blunts were successful, returning to England with six Arabian mares. With these horses they began the Crabbet Arabian Stud farm. In time, they acquired an additional 16 Arabian stallions and 51 mares. Crabbet became a legend in the world of Arabian horse breeding. Lady Anne wrote classic studies of Arabian horses along with engaging travel narratives.

At the age of 77, Lady Anne could still vault unassisted onto a horse. She died in Cairo in December 1917. Sir Wilfrid died on the Crabett estate in 1922.

WAR AND EXPLORATION

From the eighteenth century until the early twentieth century, the European exploration of Arabia was largely influenced by the rise of the Wahhabi movement and the Saud dynasty, the declining fortunes of the Ottoman Empire, and dynastic and tribal warfare. This political landscape changed dramatically between the outbreak of World War I in 1914 and the peace settlement signed between the Allies and the Ottoman Empire in 1920. The Ottomans joined the war on the side of Germany in October 1914, making enemies of Great Britain, the British Empire, and France. The British had not planned to fight the Ottomans, but they had no choice after October, given that they had become dependent on oil in the Ottoman territories in the Middle East. Most important, the British Royal Navy switched from coal to oil in fueling its ships after 1909, and it had begun to draw most of this oil from Persia. In response to the Ottoman declaration of war, the British captured virtually all the Ottoman territories in the Middle East by the end of 1917. The British also helped to organize a revolt by Arabs against the Ottomans after June 1916. The revolt was led by the ruler of the Hejaz, Sharif Husayn, who was a Hashimite with aspirations to rule all of Arabia. The Arab forces were assisted by T. E. Lawrence, who led Arab guerrillas in attacks on Turkish forces and installations. After the war, as before, Lawrence would return to Britain to consult with two of his idols, Charles Doughty and Sir Wilfrid Blunt.

Harry St. John Bridger Philby was sent to Riyadh in 1917. His task was to persuade Ibn Saud, the head of the Saud dynasty, to fight against the Ottomans. The two men struck up a friendship and came up with a plan to show the strength of the Saudis. Philby's superiors had told him that he could not travel west because the land was too dangerous. The Saudi king arranged for a camel caravan and an armed escort to take Philby across the peninsula anyway. This was a political stunt. It was also the southernmost European crossing of the peninsula to date. In 1918, Philby undertook another expedition, surveying the peninsula all the way south to the northern edge of the Empty Quarter.

The British supported the power of the Hashemites in the Hejaz after the war, provoking strong criticism from Philby. He was thoroughly devoted to Ibn Saud and thought he was Arabia's best hope for political stability. In protest against British policy, Philby resigned from the colonial service in 1925 and became a merchant in Jeddha. After crushing a civil war among Wahhabi groups, Saud declared the kingdom of Saudi Arabia in 1932. He unified the Hejaz and the Nejd for the

After conquering most of the Arabian Peninsula, Abdul Aziz al Saud, referred to as Ibn Saud, founded Saudi Arabia in 1932. During his rule (1932–1953) he changed a group of desert sheikdoms into a politically unified kingdom.

first time in centuries. Over the next decade, Philby helped open Saudi Arabia to oil exploration by U.S. companies. The peninsula's oil brought the Saudi dynasty spectacular wealth after World War II.

Philby was pleased to assist the king. However, he wanted to achieve fame as an explorer. He saw in Saudi Arabia's Empty Quarter the last blank space on the world's map. Since 1925, Philby had been attempting to get Saud's approval for the first crossing of the Empty Quarter but Saud had been busy with civil wars and other burdens. In the meantime, in 1931, Bertram Thomas completed the first crossing of the Empty Quarter. This startling achievement caused Philby to lock himself in a room for a week in despair.

Philby may not have been the first European to cross the Empty Quarter, but his explorations of the region were the most thorough. On his first successful crossing, during which he carefully surveyed his route, he took the longest and most grueling route available. After proceeding south into the Empty Quarter to Nayfah, he then led his expedition west, more than 1,250 miles (2,011 km), to Mecca. In the process of achieving fame as an explorer, Philby assisted Ibn Saud in mapping his new kingdom.

By the 1930s, the primary motives of European exploration in the Arabian Peninsula were adventure and an intense desire for fame. In the years between the two world wars, exploration on the peninsula was largely approved and directed not by European governments but by Arab rulers. They used the explorers' findings to serve their own political objectives. The next great era of exploration would be geological. The Saudi royal family would turn from Europeans to Americans for assistance. The creation of the Arabian American Oil Company, facilitated by Philby in the service of the Saudis, set the stage for aggressive oil exploration on the peninsula. Oil exploration has proceeded under the firm political control of the Saudis, who have built fortunes upon oil since the 1950s. This new era of exploration on the Arabian Peninsula was not a legacy of European imperial exploration, but rather a product of Ibn Saud's extraordinary ability to manipulate the British Empire and one of its most talented explorers to serve his own ends.

7

Exploring the Top of the World

THE HIMALAYAN PEOPLES OF TIBET AND NEPAL AT FIRST THOUGHT the European mountaineers were crazy. They could not understand why Europeans would risk death to climb the highest mountain peaks. These people had no choice but to travel among the mountains every day. Their goal was to find the lowest and easiest passes through which to bring their herds of yaks to grazing grounds, to conduct their trade, and to maintain relations with neighboring villages. For the Himalayan peoples, the mountains were significant not because they were tall but because they were the homes of the gods. They never intruded upon the homes of the gods. Instead, they would walk around the bases of the sacred mountains to show their respect.

Mountaineering in the Himalayas involved climbers from many countries, but the British clearly took the lead until 1950. The British initially were drawn into the Himalayas not by a passion for mountaineering but by their imperial competition with Russia, known as the Great Game. The Himalayas, which extend for about 1,500 miles (2,414 km), were a crucial boundary between the British Empire in India and the Russian Empire to the north. The British needed to defend this border. They sent Indian surveyors, called pundits, to map the Himalayas after the 1860s, despite the objections of the governments of Nepal and Tibet. The surveyor-general of India, Andrew Waugh, reported in 1856 that Peak XV of the Himalayas was the highest mountain known to man. It was 29,002 feet (457 m) tall. This peak is known today as Mount Everest.

Europeans regarded the discovery of the highest mountain in the world as a valuable piece of geographical information, but this information had no other obvious significance. The summit of Everest had no strategic value, and it certainly offered no hope for economic gain or colonial settlement. Moreover, at this time, the pressing interests of European geographers and explorers lay elsewhere, primarily in the rivers of Africa. By the turn of the century, however, the significance of the Himalayan peaks would begin to change and attract the interest of not only mountaineers but also British government officials.

In 1887, Lieutenant Francis Younghusband made his remarkable journey from Peking in China to India. As he approached India, he became the first European to travel through the Mustagh Pass. In his book, *Everest: The Challenge*, he recalled,

The Himalayan mountain system is home to the highest peaks in the world. There are more than 100 mountains that exceed 23,662 feet (7,200 meters). The Himalayan peoples consider many of the peaks to be the homes of the gods.

As I was ascending the valley which led up to the Mustagh Pass . . . there suddenly came into view a sight which brought me to an immediate standstill, and made me gasp with amazement. It was a mountain unbelievably higher than anything I had imagined, and I was only a few miles from its base, so that I could realize its height to the full.

I knew not what mountain it was; but I found afterwards that it was no other than K2, the second highest mountain in the world, 28,250 feet in altitude, and only 750 feet lower than Everest itself.

Two years later he returned to explore the region around K2. He later became the president of the Royal Geographical Society. He used his influence to organize the first Everest Reconnaissance Expedition in 1921.

By the start of the twentieth century, much of the map of Earth was filled in. Europeans looked for new geographical challenges, those that might not advance commerce, Christianity, or perhaps even science, but which would nonetheless symbolize the superiority of their nations. It was this change in the priorities of exploration that enabled George Mallory to explain in 1923 that he desired to climb Everest "because it is there"—an answer that would have been incomprehensible to explorers of the nineteenth century.

Plans for climbing the highest Himalayan peaks only took shape after the armistice of World War I in 1918. The British saw the ascent of Everest, in particular, as an act that would reflect the greatness of the British nation, a greatness that was already mapped upon the postwar world. The British Empire reached its maximum size at the same time that the British launched their first expeditions to climb Everest in the 1920s. How could a mountain defy the will and skill of an empire upon which the sun never set?

EARLY EXPEDITIONS TO EVEREST

In the ensuing years, an increasing number of European mountaineers arrived in the Himalayas, with a predictable mixture of success and failure. In 1909, an Italian, the duke of the Abruzzi, arrived in Kashmir with a large expedition to climb K2. After studying the mountain for some time, the duke attempted the climb with three Italian guides, four Italian porters, and some Indian porters as well. At 20,000 feet (6,096 m) they were forced to turn back, but their failure on K2 produced two pieces of important information. First, they realized they could not possibly reach the summit of K2 in a single day, as was possible on the mountains of the Alps. Instead, climbers would have to establish a series of camps where they could spend a succession of nights before proceeding. This strategy would prove essential to the successful ascent of the highest peaks, especially Mount Everest.

Second, having retreated from K2, the duke succeeded in climbing 24,600 feet (7,498 m) toward Bride Peak. Although he and his party did not reach the peak itself at 25,110 feet (7,653 m), they set a new altitude record and thus extended the boundaries of human endurance. A physician who accompanied the expedition declared afterward that altitude was not, after all, an obstacle to the ascent of the world's tallest mountains. This prediction would appear all the more reasonable with the advent of oxygen technology for mountaineers in the 1920s. The first ascent of Everest without the assistance of oxygen technology would not take place until 1978.

The most important European mountaineer in the Himalayas before World War I was Dr. Alexander Mitchell Kellas, a lecturer in chemistry at Middlesex Hospital, who first traveled to the Himalayas in 1907. Over the next several years, he would climb mountains in Tibet, Kashmir, and Sikkim, including Mount Pauhunri at 23,180 feet (7,065 m). Kellas only traveled with Tibetans and Sherpas, the latter being from the area of the Khumbu Valley in Nepal. Kellas was struck by the remarkable strength of his porters. He conducted studies of the Tibetans and Sherpas during their climbs, testing their breathing and their heart rates at high altitudes. He concluded that these people had become acclimated to high altitudes to a greater extent than Europeans could hope to become, and he proposed that they would make ideal porters for mountaineers at the highest altitudes.

Europeans had generally relied upon other Europeans, Indians, Gurkhas, and Hindu Nepalis to act as their porters. Kellas began to train Tibetans and Sherpas in advanced climbing techniques. They quickly proved themselves to be not only superior porters but also skilled climbers. Kellas brought four Sherpas with him on the British Reconnaissance

SHERPAS

In the fifteenth or sixteenth centuries, people from southeastern Tibet migrated to the eastern Himalayas, in what is now Nepal. These people became known as the Sherpa, meaning "the people from the east." Sherpas have long played an important role in exploration and mountaineering in the Himalayas, due to their strength and endurance at high altitudes. In the early twentieth century, Europeans began to use the word *sherpa* as a general description of any porter who accompanied them on a climb, so it is sometimes difficult to determine from historical records the ethnicity of particular porters.

Historically, the Sherpas grazed yak herds and grew potatoes and barley. They saw the mountains as sacred places where the gods resided. They began working as porters for European mountaineers because they could make far more money as porters than as herders and farmers. Even as Sherpas began to climb the highest mountain peaks in the 1920s, Buddhist lamas urged them not to set foot on summits. They believed this would offend the gods. In 1938 the Himalayan Club began to award the Tiger Medal to Sherpas who climbed to the highest altitudes. According to Tenzing Tashi, the grandson of Tenzing Norgay and a climber of Everest himself, this remains, for Sherpas, the ultimate mountaineering prize.

Expedition to Everest in 1921. He died of a combination of dysentery and heart failure before reaching the base of the mountain, but his encouragement of Himalayan porters was nonetheless supported by the fine performances of his porters. After the 1920s, Sherpas would become the elite high-altitude porters of the Himalayas.

The British came to regard Mount Everest as the great prize of mountaineering, but political issues stood in their way. The government of Nepal was openly hostile to European incursions, and the Tibetans were also opposed to European advances. In response to the threat of a Tibetan alliance with the Russians, a British military expedition marched to Lhasa in 1904 and imposed the Anglo-Tibetan Convention, which gave the British privileged but limited access to Tibet in the future.

The British launched their first reconnaissance expedition to Everest in 1921. Under the leadership of Charles Howard-Bury, the goal was simply to find possible paths of ascent up the mountain. The strongest climber on the expedition was George Leigh Mallory. Mallory was a graduate of Cambridge University, a veteran of World War I, and a schoolmaster. At 35, Mallory already had a good deal of experience in climbing mountains in the Alps and the Himalayas. He was in the best physical condition of his life.

Howard-Bury sent Mallory up the Rongbuk Glacier to the mountain's north face. Mallory saw a ridge that went directly to the summit, but a series of cliffs blocked his way to the ridge. He saw a gap in the cliffs, which is now known as the North Col. He suspected that he might be able to reach the gap from another angle.

The expedition traveled around the mountain to attempt to reach the North Col from the east. As Mallory had hoped, he was then able to climb an ice fall of about 1,200 feet (365 m) to the North Col. From there he looked up the north face to Everest's summit. He was encouraged by the discovery of a seemingly direct path to the summit. This would be the approach taken by the first two British expeditions to attempt to climb Everest.

In 1922, the British sent their second expedition to Everest. The goal this time was to reach the summit by climbing the north ridge. The expedition was led by Charles Bruce, who had first proposed climbing Everest in 1893. It included 40 Sherpas, in addition to local porters and 300 pack animals. The expedition did not reach the summit. However, a team of climbers using oxygen reached 27,300 feet (8,321 m), a new altitude record. Another team without oxygen reached 26,800 feet (8,168 m).

The 1922 expedition experienced the full range of dangers on Everest. The most obvious obstacle was the terrain of Everest itself, steep and often unstable, threatening an avalanche from above one's head or below one's feet. One avalanche carried nine Sherpas over an ice cliff and into a deep crevasse. Two miraculously survived long enough to be dug out of the snow. Seven died.

The mountain was also hit by sudden storms. They rose from a blue sky and proceeded quickly to hurricane conditions. Some climbers compared the wind on Everest to the lashes of a whip. The wind knocked many climbers off their feet. It brought blinding snow, forcing climbers to crawl on their hands and knees. The subzero temperatures on the mountain caused frostbite. Climbers often spoke of the peculiar feeling of numbness taking over their bodies, or their difficulty in breathing due to the cold. The cold also created problems with food. Even insulated thermoses could not keep liquids from freezing. The cold made it difficult to boil water on the climbers' primus stoves, which were also frequently used to thaw frozen boots in the mornings. The final obstacle was the lack of oxygen at altitudes over 24,000 feet (7,315 m). This caused depression, poor concentration, and a deadly condition called altitude sickness.

The 1922 climbers understood the value of oxygen. Climbing with oxygen tanks increased their speed and endurance. The climbers also learned that their bodies could get used to the higher altitudes in time. Previously, scientists thought that the body would become weaker as it remained at a high altitude. In fact, the reverse appeared to be true. The expedition also learned that they would have to pitch their final camp much closer to the summit. George Mallory had planned to locate the last camp at about 25,000 feet (7,620 m). This left an impossibly long 4,000-foot (1,219-m) dash to the summit on a single day. In later attempts on Everest, a high priority would be placed upon establishing and supplying a final camp at a much higher altitude.

A second British expedition under the leadership of Charles Bruce attempted to reach the summit of Everest in 1924. In light of their experience two years before, the British ascended the north ridge and pushed the limits of the Sherpas' endurance to place their last camp, Camp VI, closer to the summit at 26,800 feet (8,168 m). Two teams would attempt to reach the summit. Howard Somervell and Edward Norton would go first. George Mallory and Sandy Irvine would make the second attempt.

On June 5, Somervell and Norton made their bid for the summit. Their path along the north ridge was blocked by a sheer rock face. They attempted to go around the obstacle, working their way along the side of the mountain. The men balanced upon snow-covered slabs of rock that slanted like the tiles of a roof. It was a dangerous path. If one of the men fell there was nothing to break his fall to a glacier 10,000 feet (3,048 m) below.

Somervell grew tired and gave up. Norton went on alone to 28,126 feet (8,572 m). He was still short of the base of the final pyramid that caps the mountain. Fatigue and the late hour of the day finally made Norton turn back. He knew that if he kept going, he would die on the mountain. He met with Somervell, who waited on the ridge beyond the icy slabs of rock, and the men made it back to Camp IV. Due to his physical excursions at extreme altitude, Norton experienced intense pain in his eyes and went blind for 60 hours. He was still blind when he shook the hands of Mallory and Irvine as they began the expedition's second assault on the summit.

Mallory and Irvine were an odd pair. Whereas Mallory was an accomplished climber and the most fit man on the expedition, Irvine was much younger and had little previous experience in mountaineering. The men began their assault on the summit on June 8, as their colleagues nervously waited below. One of these colleagues, Noel Odell, watched them climb from far below. He saw the clouds clear on the summit and two figures moving along the ridge beneath the final summit pyramid. As Odell recalls in E. F. Norton's book, *The Fight for Everest: 1924*:

> *I noticed far away on a snow slope leading up to what seemed to me to be the last step but one from the base of the final pyramid, a tiny object moving and approaching the rock step. A second object followed, and then the first climbed to the top of the step. As I stood intently watching this dramatic appearance, the scene became enveloped in cloud once more. . . .*

Odell continued his climb to Camp VI, which he reached as a severe storm suddenly broke upon the mountain. He waited to assist Mallory and Irvine, but they did not return to Camp VI. He descended to Camp V, then returned to Camp VI two days later, finding everything just as he had left it. Upon returning to Camp V, Odell signaled to his colleagues below at Camp III, who could see Camp V through a telescope. He placed six blankets in the form of a cross, signaling "Death." The remaining members of the expedition were unable to locate and recover the bodies of Mallory and Irvine. The men were mourned in Britain as national heroes.

People have debated whether Mallory and Irvine reached the summit of Everest. It is improbable. They used primitive equipment, and they were hit by the sudden storm witnessed by Odell. Despite this, many people hoped for some future proof of their success. Later climbers looked for any sign left by Mallory and Irvine on the summit but found nothing. Mallory's body was finally found in 1999. It was frozen face down to a slope beneath the precarious rock tiles. His remains told little about his success or failure in his attempt to reach the summit. He had broken his leg in a fall, and there was still a rope tied around his waist. The rope suggested that he and Irvine had been joined in their fate. Irvine's body has yet to be found.

REACHING THE SUMMIT

Since 1921, the British had been approaching Everest from the north through Tibet. This approach was difficult. Climbers had to pass through barren lands and high mountain passes. Now they saw the possibility of approaching the mountain through Nepal. In October 1950, Communist China invaded and took over Tibet. This international crisis then produced an unexpected benefit for British mountaineers. Fears of Chinese expansion had caused Nepal to open its borders to Europeans for the first time. The approach through Nepal was easier on the climbers. They traveled through farm lands and beautiful forests. The altitude rose gradually. This helped the mountaineers in acclimatizing. Moreover, the approach through Nepal brought expeditions through the Khumbu valley. Everest stood at the head of this valley. It was also the home of the Sherpas.

The Nepalese government authorized a Swiss expedition to make an assault on Everest in 1952. Ed Wyss-Dunant led this expedition. Wyss-Dunant then hired a Sherpa named Tenzing Norgay to be the *sirdar*, or head of the expedition's porters. Tenzing was 38 and had been to Everest with earlier British and Swiss expeditions. It was Tenzing and Raymond Lambert who made the expedition's final assault on Everest's summit in May 1952. They reached 28,210 feet (8,598 m) before the bad weather turned them back.

The British mountaineers were relieved that the Swiss had failed in their attempt to climb Everest. The Nepalese government had given them permission to make the next assault in 1953. They knew they

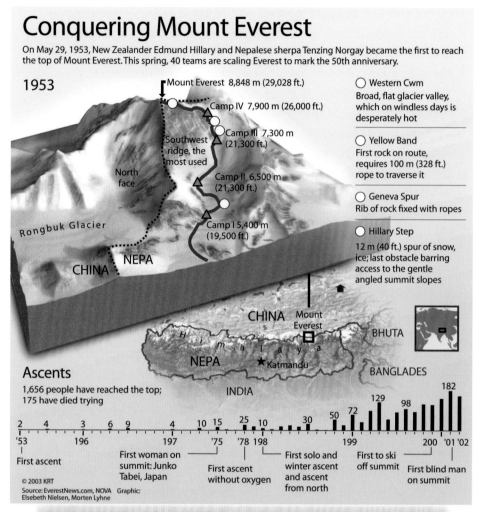

Conquering Mount Everest

On May 29, 1953, New Zealander Edmund Hillary and Nepalese sherpa Tenzing Norgay became the first to reach the top of Mount Everest. This spring, 40 teams are scaling Everest to mark the 50th anniversary.

1953

Mount Everest 8,848 m (29,028 ft.)

Camp IV 7,900 m (26,000 ft.)

Camp III 7,300 m (21,300 ft.)

Southwest ridge, the most used

North face

Camp II 6,500 m (21,300 ft.)

Rongbuk Glacier

Camp I 5,400 m (19,500 ft.)

NEPA

CHINA

○ Western Cwm
Broad, flat glacier valley, which on windless days is desperately hot

○ Yellow Band
First rock on route, requires 100 m (328 ft.) rope to traverse it

○ Geneva Spur
Rib of rock fixed with ropes

○ Hillary Step
12 m (40 ft.) spur of snow, ice; last obstacle barring access to the gentle angled summit slopes

CHINA Mount Everest

BHUTA

H i m a l a y a

NEPA ★Katmandu

BANGLADES

INDIA

Ascents

1,656 people have reached the top; 175 have died trying

2 4 3 6 9 4 10 15 25 10 30 50 72 129 98 182

'53 196 197 '75 '78 198 199 200 '01 '02

First ascent

First woman on summit: Junko Tabei, Japan

First ascent without oxygen

First solo and winter ascent and ascent from north

First to ski off summit

First blind man on summit

© 2003 KRT

Source: EverestNews.com, NOVA Graphic:
Elsebeth Nielsen, Morten Lyhne

On May 29, 1953, Edmund Hillary and Sherpa Tenzing Norgay became the first to reach the summit of Mount Everest. This graphic shows the route.

had to succeed this time. If they failed, the French would have the next opportunity to climb Everest in 1954 and the Swiss would try again in 1955. Moreover, the British were crowning a new queen, Elizabeth II, in June 1953. They hoped to celebrate the coronation with the first successful ascent to the top of the world.

Under the leadership of John Hunt, a former army officer, the expedition set up its base camp near the foot of the southwest face of the mountain. It then established a series of eight camps. Two assault teams and one team of porters would try to reach the mountain's summit from Camp VIII. The first team was Charles Evans and Tom Bourdillon. They made their bid for the summit on May 26. Evans and Bourdillon climbed toward the summit along the southeast ridge. They became the first to reach what is called the South Summit of Everest. This peak stands below the main peak. They attempted to push on, but due to intense fatigue and the late hour of the day, they were forced to turn back. They had stopped just several hundred feet short of their goal.

Edmund Hillary and Tenzing Norgay made up the second assault team. On May 28, they set off toward the southeast ridge with the support team of George Lowe, Alf Gregory, and Ang Nyima. Hillary was now carrying more than 60 pounds (27 kilograms), and each of the other men carried about 50 pounds (22 kg). They proceeded to 27,900 feet (8,503 m), where they established Camp IX. All but Hillary and Tenzing returned down the mountain.

That night the two men ate chicken-noodle soup, canned apricots, and a hot lemon drink before going to sleep. They awoke at 4:00 A.M. The temperature was –27°C (–80.6°F). Hillary's boots were frozen, so he thawed them over their stove before attaching his crampons (a set of steel spikes that strap on to the soles of shoes for better traction on ice). Hillary and Tenzing set off at 6:30 A.M. They were slowed by "breakable crust," snow that has a thin, hard layer on top. A climber can break through the crust and fall up to his or her knee or waist in soft snow beneath. Fortunately, the terrain hardened as they reached the South Summit. The men continued along the summit ridge.

Hillary went first, cutting steps into the icy snow. The men climbed this as a staircase toward the summit, which they could not yet see. Within just a few hundred feet of the summit, a rock face blocked their path. Hillary saw, to the right of the rock face, a large crack between the rock and a huge piece of ice hanging over the ridge. Hillary wanted to climb through the crack but there was a danger that the ice would break away from the rock, leaving him to fall thousands of feet down the face of the mountain. Hillary moved into the crack, facing the rock. He describes his climb in his memoir, *View from the Summit*:

I jammed my crampons into the ice behind me and then wriggled my way upward using every little handhold I could find. Puffing for breath, I made steady height—the ice was holding—and forty feet up I pulled myself out of the crack onto the top of the rock face. I had made it!

Hillary helped Tenzing to climb through the crack. He then used his ice axe to cut more steps upward. "Next moment I had moved onto a flattish exposed area of snow with nothing but space in every direction," Hillary recalls. "Tenzing quickly joined me and we looked around in wonder. To our immense satisfaction, we realized we had reached the top of the world!" It was 11:30 A.M.

Hillary extended his hand in a formal manner to his partner. Tenzing instead gave him a strong bear hug in celebration. Hillary removed his oxygen mask. He took out his camera and photographed Tenzing on the summit. Tenzing held his ice axe aloft with the flags of the United Nations, India, Nepal, and Great Britain fluttering in the stiff wind. Hillary then took pictures down every side of the mountain as proof of their achievement. Before they began their descent, Tenzing left bits of chocolate, cookies, and a pencil as gifts for the gods.

EXPLORATION FROM EVEREST TO SPACE

The leaders of the British expedition to Everest hoped to declare their triumph before the coronation of Queen Elizabeth II in June 1953. They succeeded, and the conquest of Everest was announced in *The Times* of London on June 2. This was the day on which Elizabeth was crowned.

The presence of Tenzing on the summit of Everest challenged the long-standing leadership of Europeans in exploration. This challenge became apparent during the celebration of the conquest of Everest. As the members of the expedition approached Kathmandu, the capital of Nepal, Tenzing, Hillary, and Hunt (the expedition's leader) were placed in a jeep. Nepali officials told Hillary and Hunt to sit. They told Tenzing to stand, balancing himself upon the jeep's roll bar. They then proceeded into the capital, where Tenzing was cheered wildly as a national hero. To Hillary's annoyance, there were banners along the roads that pictured Tenzing atop Everest. The pictures showed him holding a rope

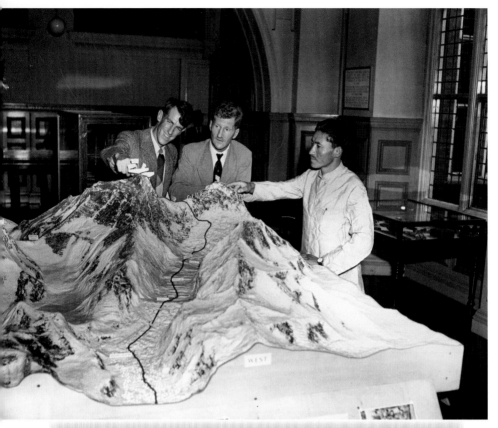

Following their successful ascent to the top of Mount Everest, (*left to right*) Edmund Hillary, John Hunt (leader of the expedition), and Tenzing Norgay became world famous. Here at a press conference at the Royal Geographical Society in London, the men describe their climb to the top of the world.

attached to a white man, who lay on his back with his feet and arms in the air. King Tribhuvan introduced the three men to the people. He stated that Tenzing had reached the summit of Everest first. In fact, Hillary had led the way to the summit; however, he and Tenzing had told the king that they had arrived on the summit together.

When the expedition arrived in Delhi, Tenzing was again hailed as the hero of the Everest climb. He was identified as a resident of India in an attempt to gain fame for India. In the era of decolonization that followed World War II, exploration was no longer a triumphant story of European heroics. It was a source of pride for non-Europeans who wished to mark their own achievements as independent nations.

Tenzing's climb marked another global development. One of the flags that he held aloft on his ice axe was the flag of the United Nations. He thus claimed the top of the world not only for particular nations but also for all humankind. The remarkable potential of international cooperation in exploration is now being demonstrated on another frontier: the planets and stars beyond Earth. The *International Space Station* is the largest coordinated scientific undertaking in human history. It is an exploratory mission like none other before it.

Today exploration is identified, above all, with space, although there continue to be important explorations of the deep ocean floors, which remain largely unknown. It is a quest for scientific knowledge, commercial benefits, strategic advantages, and national prestige. Yet the future might offer a new era in exploration. Humans might someday settle in space. If that happens, it remains to be seen whether countries will make new claims to territory. One wonders if space will be divided in the name of commerce, religion, or the nation. How this comes to pass may determine whether people have entered a new era of exploration after all.

Chronology

1492   Queen Isabella and King Ferdinand of Spain hire Italian sea captain Christopher Columbus to find a western sea route to Asia. On October 12, Columbus lands on an island in the Caribbean and names it San Salvador.

1493   Pope Alexander VI issues papal bull, "donating" the lands on one side of the globe to Spain (the New World) and lands on the other side to Portugal (Africa and the East). The Treaty

Timeline

1497–1498
Portugal gains control of spice routes

1520
Ferdinand Magellan finds westward route to Spice Islands for Spain

1813–1907
British Empire and Russian Empire battle for supremacy in central Asia. This period is referred to as the Great Game

1494   1856

1494
Treaty of Tordesillas enforces Pope Alexander's papal bull, dividing the globe between Spain and Portugal

17th century
Dutch, English, and French ignore papal bull of 1493 and establish trading posts in the East. Portugal's and Spain's powers weaken

1849–1856
David Livingstone becomes first European to cross the width of southern Africa

of Tordesillas, which enforces the papal bull, is signed on June 7, 1494.

1497–1498 Vasco da Gama becomes the first navigator to find a route to India around Africa's Cape of Good Hope. Gives Portugal control of spice routes.

1520 Ferdinand Magellan is commissioned by Spain to find westward route to Spice Islands. His expedition is the first to circumnavigate the globe, but he does not survive the journey.

17th century Dutch, English, and French ignore papal bull of 1493 and establish trading posts in the East. Portugal's and Spain's powers weaken.

1875
Verney Lovett Cameron becomes first European to travel across Africa from east to west

1862
William Gifford Palgrave becomes first European to travel eastward across the Arabian Peninsula

1953
Edmund Hillary and Tenzing Norgay become first to reach the summit of Mount Everest

1858   1953

1858
John Hanning Speke locates the source of the Nile River—Lake Victoria

1932
Ibn Saud unites various territories on the Arabian Peninsula and renames it Saudi Arabia

1813–1907	British Empire and Russian Empire battle for supremacy in central Asia. This period is referred to as the Great Game.
1830	Royal Geographical Society is founded in London. It becomes the key supporter of many famous explorers and expeditions.
1849–1856	First expedition of David Livingstone to find the upper Zambezi River. In 1855, he finds and names Victoria Falls. He becomes the first European to cross the width of southern Africa.
1858–1863	Second expedition of David Livingstone to explore eastern and central Africa. His goal is to establish mission stations on the Batoka Plateau. It is considered a failure.
1858	John Hanning Speke locates the source of the Nile River—Lake Victoria.
1862	William Gifford Palgrave becomes first European to travel eastward across the Arabian Peninsula.
1865–1873	Third and final expedition of David Livingstone. His goal is to find the source of the Nile River. He dies in May 1873 of dysentery. His heart and internal organs are removed and buried at the foot of a tree; his body is shipped back to Britain and buried in Westminster Abbey.
1871	Henry Morton Stanley hired to find David Livingstone. Upon finding the disheveled Livingstone near Lake Tanganyika in present-day Tanzania, he utters the famous phrase, "Dr. Livingstone, I presume?"
1874	Henry Morton Stanley hired to trace the course of the River Congo to the sea. Only 114 out of 356 survive of which Stanley is the only European.
1875	Verney Lovett Cameron becomes the first European to travel across Africa from east to west.
1887	Francis Younghusband journeys from Peking, China, to India. He becomes the first European to travel through the Mustagh Pass.

1924   On his third expedition to Mount Everest, George Mallory and his climbing partner, Andrew Irvine, disappear on the northeast ridge.

1932   Ibn Saud unites various territories on the Arabian Peninsula and renames it Saudi Arabia.

1953   Edmund Hillary and Tenzing Norgay become the first to reach the summit of Mount Everest.

Glossary

abolitionist—An opponent of slavery.

bodhisattva—According to Buddhists, this is a person who has earned nirvana, but who has chosen to remain on earth in order to assist others in the quest for spiritual truth.

bedouin—Nomadic groups of people in the Nejd.

calico—A simple, inexpensive cotton fabric.

Cathay—An ancient European name for the region of present-day China.

conquistador—A Spanish soldier.

cornice—An ice formation hanging over a ridge.

crampons—Steel spikes that attach to boots for better traction on ice.

Dalai Lama—The spiritual and political leader of Tibet.

dysentery—A potentially fatal disease of the intestines.

emir—A Muslim ruler in Central Asia.

ghazú—A Bedouin raiding party.

hajj—The Muslim pilgrimage to Mecca.

Iberian Peninsula—The region of present-day Spain and Portugal.

khan—A Muslim ruler in Central Asia.

Khoikhoi—Peoples of South Africa who lived in clans and supported themselves by herding cattle and fat-tailed sheep.

nirvana—According to Buddhists, this is the state of eternal tranquility that follows one's release from reincarnation.

papal dominion—The authority of the pope to determine sovereignty over land.

pundit—A learned Indian who conducted surveys or other forms of exploration in the service of the British in India.

raja—A Hindu ruler in Asia.

San—Peoples of South Africa who lived along the coast as hunter-gatherers.

Sherpas—A people of Tibetan origin who live primarily in the Khumbu region of Nepal.

sirdar—A leader among the porters of Himalayan climbs.

Bibliography

Alder, Garry. *Beyond Bokhara: The Life of William Moorcroft*. London: Century Publishing, 1985.

Breashears, David, et al. *Last Climb: The Legendary Everest Expeditions of George Mallory*. New York: National Geographic, 1999.

Crosby, Alfred. *The Columbian Exchange*. New York: Praeger, 2003.

——. *Ecological Imperialism*. Cambridge: Cambridge University Press, 1993.

Curtin, Philip. *The World and the West*. Cambridge: Cambridge University Press, 2002.

——. *Disease and Empire*. Cambridge: Cambridge University Press, 1998.

Diamond, Jared. *Guns, Germs, and Steel*. New York: W. W. Norton & Co., 1999.

Geniesse, Jane Fletcher. *Passionate Nomad: The Life of Freya Stark*. New York: Random House, 2001.

Hillary, Edmund. *View from the Summit*. New York: Pocket Books, 1999.

Hopkirk, Peter. *Quest for Kim*. Ann Arbor: University of Michigan Press, 1999.

——. *The Great Game*. New York: Kodansha International, 1994.

Jeal, Tim. *Livingstone*. New Haven: Yale University Press, 2001.

Keay, John. *The Great Arc: The Dramatic Tale of How India Was Mapped and Everest Was Named*. New York: HarperPerennial, 2000.

——. *The Gilgit Game: The Explorers of the Western Himalayas, 1865–95*. Oxford: Oxford University Press, 1993.

——. *The Mammoth Book of Explorers*. New York: Caroll & Graf, 2002.

——. *The Royal Geographical Society History of World Exploration*. London: Hamlyn, 1991.

McLynn, Frank. *Hearts of Darkness: The European Exploration of Africa*. New York: Carroll & Graf Publishers, 1992.

Moorehead, Alan. *The White Nile*. New York: HarperPerennial, 2000.

——. *The Blue Nile*. New York: HarperPerennial, 2000.

——. The *Fatal Impact: The Invasion of the South Pacific, 1767–1840*. New York: HarperCollins, 1990.

National Portrait Gallery. *David Livingstone and the Victorian Encounter with Africa*. London: National Portrait Gallery Publications, 1996.

Pakenham, Thomas. *The Scramble for Africa*. New York: Avon Books, 1992.

Rice, Edward. *Captain Sir Richard Francis Burton: A Biography*. New York: DaCapo Press, 2001.

Roberts, David, and Jan Morris. *Great Exploration Hoaxes*. New York: Modern Library, 2001.

Shipman, Pat. *To the Heart of the Nile: Lady Florence Baker and the Exploration of Central Africa*. New York: William Morrow, 2003.

Slung, Michele. *Living with Cannibals and Other Women's Adventures*. New York: National Geographic, 2001.

Sobel, Dava. *Longitude*. New York: Penguin USA, 1996.

Stark, Freya. *The Valleys of the Assassins*. New York: Modern Library, 2001.

Tenzing, Tashi. *Tenzing Norgay and the Sherpas of Everest*. Camden, Maine: Ragged Mountain Press, 2001.

Unsworth, Walt. *Everest: The Mountaineering History*. Seattle: The Mountaineers, 2000.

Further Resources

FICTION

Kingsolver, Barbara. *The Poisonwood Bible*. New York: HarperPerennial, 1999.

Kipling, Rudyard. *Kim*. New York: Viking Press, 1992.

Swift, Jonathan. *Gulliver's Travels*. New York: Penguin Press, 2003.

DVD

Khartoum (1966). MGM/UA Video, DVD, 2002.

Lawrence of Arabia (1962). Columbia Tri-Star, DVD, 2001.

The Mission (1986). Warner Studios, DVD, 1995.

CD-ROM

Richard Burton's Arabian Nights and Victorian Books of Exploration and Travel in Asia and Africa. B & R Samizdat Express, 2002.

WEB SITES

Hakluyt Society
http://www.hakluyt.com/hak-soc-links.htm
This site provides links to other sites containing detailed research materials on exploration and navigation. It also includes sites with up-to-date news about forthcoming events, conferences, and exhibits.

National Geographic Society Xpeditions
http://www.nationalgeographic.com/expeditions/
Home to the U.S. National Geography Standards. Includes a wealth of resources for teachers and students, such as lesson plans, maps, and classroom activities.

Royal Geographic Society Education Resources
http://www.rgs.org/SpecialInterests/students/Students.htm
Established in 1830, this organization is the largest and most active scholarly geographical society in the world. Students and teachers can use the site as a resource for events, exhibits, and lesson planning.

Society for the History of Discoveries
http://sochistdisc.org/links.htm
Links to sites about the discovery, exploration, and mapping of the world from earliest times to the present.

United States Library of Congress Geography and Map Reading Room
http://loc.gov/rr/geogmap/gmpage.html
The Geography and Map Division of the Library of Congress has custody of the largest cartographic collection in the world, including 5.5 million maps, 80,000 atlases, 6,000 reference works, over 500 globes and globe gores, 3,000 raised relief models, and other cartographic materials in different formats.

United States Library of Congress Meeting of Frontiers
http://frontiers.loc.gov/intldl/mtfhtml/mfhome.html
A bilingual multimedia English-Russian digital library that tells the story of American exploration and settlement of the West, the exploration and settlement of Siberia and the Russian Far East, and the meeting of the Russian-American frontier in Alaska and the Pacific Northwest.

Picture Credits

Index

About the Contributors

Author **KEVIN PATRICK GRANT** holds an A.B. with high honors in history from the University of California, Berkeley, an M.A. in history from the University of Chicago, and a Ph.D. from the University of California, Berkeley. He is an associate professor at Hamilton College and the author of *A Civilised Savagery: Britain and the New Slaveries in Africa, 1884–1926* and a variety of essays on the history of the British Empire.

General editor **JOHN S. BOWMAN** received a B.A. in English literature from Harvard University and matriculated at Trinity College, Cambridge University, as Harvard's Fiske Scholar and at the University of Munich. Bowman has worked as an editor and as a freelance writer for more than 40 years. He has edited numerous works of history, as well as served as general editor of Chelsea House's AMERICA AT WAR set. Bowman is the author of more than 10 books, including a volume in this series, *Exploration in the World of the Ancients, Revised Edition.*

General editor **MAURICE ISSERMAN** holds a B.A. in history from Reed College and an M.A. and Ph.D. in history from the University of Rochester. He is a professor of history at Hamilton College, specializing in twentieth-century U.S. history and the history of exploration. Isserman was a Fulbright distinguished lecturer at Moscow State University. He is the author of 12 books.